Histori

FROM COLLECTIONS IN

Merseyside County Museums

© Merseyside County Museums 1979
ISBN 0 85331 418 7

Printed by Wood Westworth & Co Ltd, St Helens, Lancs

Contents

Foreword

The idea of presenting an exhibition of historic glass in Merseyside County Museums first arose in the summer of 1978 when it became known that the Association Internationale pour l'Histoire du Verre were intending to visit Merseyside in September 1979 as part of the programme for their Eighth Congress. It seemed therefore a particularly appropriate occasion on which to try to bring together some of the finest examples of historic glass from public collections in North West England

The two hundred and fifty objects chosen for the exhibition provide a rich, varied and fascinating commentary on the functional and decorative aspects of glassware from the time of the Egyptian New Kingdom to the flourishing of Art Nouveau in America. The exhibitio amply demonstrates the debt which we owe to a number of prominent antiquarians and collectors living in the North West of England during the Victorian and Edwardian periods whose connoisseurship and generous bequests have so richly endowed our public collections.

It is unlikely that such a comprehensive selection of historic glass will be seen again in this region for many years and it is intended therefore that the exhibition and the accompanying catalogue should provide a full assessment of the significance that our collections in the North West hold for the study of historic glass in general.

Richard Foster
Director
Merseyside County Museums

Acknowledgements

Introduction	Ian Wolfenden (with notes on some collectors supplied by Anthea Jarvis and Margaret Warhurst)
Section A	Margaret Warhurst
Section B	Margaret Warhurst
Section C	Margaret Warhurst and Lionel Burman
Section D	Anthea Jarvis and Ian Wolfenden
Section E	Anthea Jarvis
Section F	Ian Wolfenden
Section G	Anthea Jarvis and Ian Wolfenden
Editor	Ian Wolfenden

The authors of the catalogue wish to acknowledge the assistance of
D.B. Harden, J. Price, I. Burgoyne, Mrs C. Gray and Mrs D. Clarke.

Photography

All photographs have been taken by Merseyside County Museums
photographers, Colin Pitcher and David Flower, with the exception
of the following:

G2, G5, G6, G7, G8, G9, G11, G12	R.L. Bell, Manchester Polytechnic
G10, G15, G16	History of Art Dept, University of Manchester
A1, A4, A5, A12, A17, A26, A28, A29, A32, A34, A35, A39, A40, A41, A42, A45, A47, C3, C5	The Manchester Museum
A15, A19, A22, C1, D2, D3, D5, D9, D10, D12, D17, D22, D30, D31, E1, E3, F2, F11, F14, F17, G1, G24	Pilkington Glass Museum
F7, F8, F9	J.W. Stammers AIIP, Central University Photographic Service, University of Liverpool
D35	T. Wilson and Son, Kendal
Design of Exhibition	Jon Hall, Susan Ollerenshaw
Design of Catalogue	Sarah Roughsedge, Allan Hope, Barrie Jones

Introduction

Glass has long held a fascination for collectors. Of the Roman Emperor Tacitus it was said that 'he had a passion for glass, its diversity and intricate workmanship.'(1) In the Middle Ages its resemblance to precious stones caused it to be prized and stored in Cathedral treasuries. The enlightenment which accompanied the Renaissance brought renewed interest in its aesthetic and technical qualities and the great glass industry of Venice was stimulated by the study of ancient Roman vessels. Knowledge of the history of glass remained slight until the nineteenth century, when the classification of the subject began to be undertaken in earnest. In England Apsley Pellatt's 'Curiosities of Glassmaking' (1849) was an early attempt to trace the development of the craft. By the middle of the century collections of glass could be formed on the basis of a general understanding of glass history. This period also saw the establishment of the Museum of Ornamental Art at South Kensington and the foundation of public museums throughout the country. The glass collections of the Early Victorian age, both private and public, were part of a widespread movement to preserve evidence of past skills for present instruction and delight.

In north-west England the first important showing of historic glass was at the Manchester Art Treasures Exhibition of 1857. The exhibition, modelled in some respects on the Great Exhibition of 1851, brought together many works of art, both fine and applied. Glass took its place in the 'Museum of Ornamental Art', an area of the exhibition which, in the words of a contemporary critic, was 'calculated to produce the most practically useful result, and to be of the highest importance to the community.'(2) Mid-nineteenth century writers stressed the value of placing historical models before the public, particularly in manufacturing districts, and it was doubtless felt appropriate that Venetian and German glass, Dutch glass and Islamic should be displayed in a city notable for the production of high quality tableware. Since the time of the Manchester exhibition the north-west has declined as a producer of tableglass and its glass collections have been formed more through enlightened self-interest than from a sense of communal values. Nevertheless it is appropriate that this traditional glassmaking area should hold some of the finest collections of glass in the provinces and that in one place at least, St Helens, it is possible to see a collection of historic glass in a town where glass is still produced.

North West Collections—the mid-nineteenth century

Prominent among the contributors to the 1857 Exhibition in Manchester was Joseph Mayer of Liverpool and in contemporary accounts of the exhibition his collections received due notice. Mayer was a man of substance and a voracious collector; in the history of collecting in the north-west he is the outstanding mid-nineteenth century figure.

Born in Staffordshire, Joseph Mayer (1803 - 1886) was apprenticed as a goldsmith to his brother-in-law in Liverpool in 1821. His interests were wide and chiefly archaeological and he collected more than 10,000 antiquities In 1852 he opened a private Egyptian Museum in Liverpool to house parts of his collection. His glass was apparently acquired incidentally among his many purchases. Thus in 1852, on a visit to Cologne, he bought Roman glass with much other material. Mostly his glass is unprovenanced but exceptional in this respect is that from the Faussett collection of Kentish antiquities purchased by Mayer in 1854. This material was excavated from Anglo-Saxon graves by the Reverend Bryan Faussett in the 1770s and was recorded in meticulously kept excavation diaries, which Mayer also obtained. Faussett unearthed a number of Teutonic glasses in Kent, of which eight (nos. B2 - 3; B7 - 11) are shown in the present exhibition. Most striking perhaps is the dark olive green claw-beaker (no. B2), which may be seen as an outstanding example of the technical skills and strong formal sense of the Dark Age glassmakers.

Ancient glass, particularly Roman, was of great interest to nineteenth century collectors. Unfortunately however we do not know Mayer's own view of his Roman and Dark Age glass. It is noteworthy that he showed none of it at the Manchester Exhibition, although he did lend Celtic and Anglo-Saxon enamels from the Faussett collection 'of the greatest beauty and interest.'(3) Early Victorian attitudes favoured ornamental art and the earliest glass shown in Manchester was an Islamic lamp, dated to the fourteenth or early fifteenth century and richly enamelled. Dexterity and industry were fashionable virtues in the mid-century and the approach to ancient and early mediaeval glass, except the more sophisticated pieces such as the Portland Vase, was generally antiquarian. A contemporary account of ancient glass like that of Apsley Pellatt in 'Curiosities of Glass-making' was still to some extent dependent upon a patchwork of references to early antiquarians such as Camden, Stow and Stukeley. One may well suspect that Mayer assembled his collection of early glass piece-meal and without the appreciation that can only accompany knowledge.

In 1867 Mayer gave the bulk of his collection to the City of Liverpool and it is now housed in the Merseyside County Museums. In addition to several hundred pieces of Egyptian, Roman and Dark Age glass the collection included items of Continental and English glass from the Late Mediaeval period to the eighteenth century. Thus Mayer established at Liverpool the basis for a collection fully representative of the history of glass. It is interesting to note that at this date the other great city of South Lancashire, Manchester, had no municipal museum and that public collections of glass and other applied arts were not formed there in any significant degree before the first decades of the twentieth century. Indeed Joseph Mayer's glass was for many years the only substantial public collection in the region as a whole.

North West Collections—the later nineteenth century
During the later nineteenth century museum rather than private collections call for comment. The concept of the Museum of Ornamental Art, as established in South Kensington in 1852 and furthered in the Manchester Exhibition of 1857, was now slowly developed in South and East Lancashire, which had strong manufacturing traditions and growing centres of population. The best glass acquired was Venetian. Venetian glass was greatly admired throughout the nineteenth century and it fetched consistently high prices. At the Lady Bagot sale at Christie's in 1840 two Venetian glasses had made £19.15s. and 10 guineas respectively while an English beaker, with a coat of arms enamelled by William Beilby of Newcastle, fetched a guinea.(4) Today the English glass would be worth perhaps ten times the equivalent Venetian pieces. The Venetian appeal lay above all in colour: 'Nothing can

be imagined more delicately beautiful than the colour of the opal glasses, tazzas etc.... and the varied iridescent tints they assume according as the light falls upon them.'(5)

In 1876 Liverpool acquired fine Venetian and façon de Venise glass for its Mayer Museum. The early sixteenth century pedestal-foot bowl (no. D1) and the latticino façon de Venise covered goblet of c1600 (no. D10) are good examples. In the same year A.W. Franks, who bequeathed much of his collection to the British Museum, presented to Liverpool a tazza of c1600 (no. D4) and a goblet in 'vetro a retorti' glass of the same date (no. D5). We have no statement of an acquisition policy in Liverpool at this period. However at a much smaller museum, the Blackburn Museum and Art Gallery, the Museum accession records and Committee minutes reveal the intention to establish collections worthy of a museum of ornamental art and devoted to the improvement of public taste. Blackburn bought a range of applied art, particularly in the 1880s, out of the profits of locally organised exhibitions. Their glass, like Liverpool's, was Venetian, although contemporary rather than renaissance or baroque (nos. F3 - 6).

North West Collections—the turn of the century

In the late Victorian and Edwardian periods glass collecting became a fashionable pastime and the first popular books on glass and glass collecting were published. Above all English glass, so much more readily available than ancient or continental, began to be appreciated, with the result that both private and public collecting were greatly stimulated.

a) Ancient and Continental glass collections

The traditional English interest in ancient and continental glass was followed by two collectors of this period - Jesse Haworth (1835 - 1921) and Leicester Collier (d. 1917). Haworth was a Lancashire manufacturer, inspired by a visit to Egypt in the early 1880s to a deep interest in Egyptian antiquities. Although no more of a specialist glass collector than Joseph Mayer, his approach to collecting reflects a new era. Rather than purchase from dealers or other collectors Haworth chose to finance excavations in Egypt, supporting Sir Flinders Petrie's work there from 1887 and aiding the Egyptian Exploration Fund. His glass thus has the merit of provenance. The gift of his antiquities from Petrie's excavations to the Manchester Museum in 1912 established the glass collection of that institution.

Leicester Collier was a Keswick man who bequeathed his collections to the Manchester City Art Galleries in 1917. Like Haworth he was not a glass specialist, collecting Oriental, Continental and English porcelain, and paintings and prints in addition to glass. His glass collection was small but broadly based. A 1918 manuscript catalogue in the gallery file notes 55 entries for glass, classified as 8 Venetian; 10 Netherlandish; 15 Dutch or English; 5 English; 9 Spanish; 7 Bohemian; 1 German and 1 French. Collier seems to have taken a certain interest in engraved glass, of which the French jug commemorating Austerlitz (no. F1) is a notable example. His collection remains the only significant holding of continental glass in Manchester.

b) English glass collections

The nineteenth century was slow to appreciate the qualities of English glass. Although by the mid-century continental, particularly Venetian glass was being keenly studied, English glass was apparently collected as much for its utillty as for its beauty. In a delightful footnote in his pioneer work on Old English Glasses, Albert Hartshorne recorded that: '...the late Mr Hartshorne and Mr Albert Way ...were, perhaps, the earliest of modern antiquaries to recognise the merits of Old English wineglasses, and used no others at their tables.'(6) Early Victorian collectors took little interest in English glass and not until the publication of Hartshorne's book in 1897 was there a serious reference work on the subject. By the end of the nineteenth century a growing awareness of the history of English glass is reflected in the formation of a number of fine collections of seventeenth and eighteenth century glass. In the present exhibition two such collections are represented - those of David Lloyd Roberts, now in the Manchester City Art Galleries, and William Malin Roscoe, now in the Merseyside County Museums. Distinguished by their comprehensiveness and by the quality of certain individual specimens, these collections remain today among the most outstanding in the north-west.

The collection of William Malin Roscoe (c1856 - 1915) is of interest as one of a number of specialist collections of English glass of the Late Victorian and Edwardian periods.(7) Roscoe spent his working life in Bristol, moving later to Herefordshire and finally to Birchamp in Gloucestershire. He collected his glasses between 1894 and 1915, especially from local sources.(8) It is possible that he intended a collection of glass of the Bristol region, although a manuscript catalogue dated 1903 and recording about half of his glass now in the Merseyside County Museums, makes no note of attribution or indeed of whence he obtained the glasses. Whether or not he searched specifically for locally made glass he certainly concentrated upon English pieces of quality. The set of twelve wines with chinoiserie engravings (no. E34) are among the most charming of surviving English eighteenth century glasses and even more finely engraved is his chinoiserie goblet (no. E33). Typical of the uniformly high quality of his collection are the glasses with baroque engraved borders (eg E24 and E25), which have no parallels in other north-west collections. After his death his glass passed to his son who added pieces to the collection, and it was bequeathed to the City of Liverpool by Mrs A.M. Roscoe in 1949.

The other specialist English collection of the period is that of David Lloyd Roberts (1834 - 1920). Lloyd Roberts was a Stockport man born in humble circumstances. He became a surgeon at St Mary's Hospital, Manchester, specialising in gynaecology. His cultural interests included the collecting of books, watercolours, oils, prints and silver in addition to glass. These he was able to collect with a freedom secured by the fortune he made from his work. Lloyd Roberts' wife died in 1910 and, in the absence of children, his collections were bequeathed in 1920 to the City of Manchester.

Of Lloyd Roberts' collecting methods we know very little. We do know that his silver collection was built up from about 1880 until the time of his death and that he bought in Manchester, London and elsewhere. A Manchester dealer who supplied him with silver described him as an 'omnivorous buyer' and stressed the catholicity of his taste. Some of his best glasses are not on show in this exhibition, a beautiful covered bowl with 'flowered' engraving for example (9), or a wine glass engraved in diamond point by David Wolff. However the giant goblet showing the infant Bacchus astride a barrel (no. E10), an early example of wheel engraving on an English glass, will suggest the interest of his collection, which has a comprehensive series of wineglasses and many other types of vessel. Today, as a public collection, its range does not perhaps seem unduly remarkable, yet it should be remembered that in 1920 the public had little opportunity to see good English glass. The catalogue to the 1921 Manchester exhibition of the Lloyd Roberts bequest noted: 'The valuable collection made by Dr David Lloyd Roberts and bequeathed by him to the City of Manchester is, up to the present time, the largest and most complete collection of Old English Glass belonging to any public museum in the Kingdom.' The claim was not without some foundation; most of the great private collections of English glass became public only in the 1920s or 1930s or indeed after the Second World War. Thus, in addition to its intrinsic merit, the Lloyd Roberts collection has particular interest for its place in the development of public collections of English glass.

c) Art glass collections

Most contemporary glass was ignored by both public and private collectors throughout the nineteenth century. English art glass, particularly the work of James Powell & Sons of London created an interest in Late Victorian glass among collectors of the period, which perhaps in certain respects paralleled the new interest in old English

glasses. In both types of glass simplicity of form and 'glassy' imperfections of fabric exercised an appeal to a generation less convinced by sheer virtuosity than its forbears. Equally, although in a different way, the art nouveau movement reflected the changes in taste around 1900 and glass in art nouveau style was immediately collected. It was again in Manchester that the new interests first found public expression.

Powell glass was perhaps first collected in Manchester by Thomas Coylan Horsfall (1841 - 1932). Horsfall was a cotton merchant who retired at forty-one to establish, under the direct inspiration of John Ruskin, a museum in the Ancoats slum area of Manchester. His Ancoats Museum had primarily an educational function, one aspect of which was to encourage a taste for good design among people who had little opportunity to afford it in their own homes. Horsfall assembled an applied art collection which included examples of glass made by the Powell firm (eg no. G4). This was transferred to the City Art Gallery in 1918, by which date the early success of the museum was over-shadowed by the growth of the City's art collections.

A more distinguished art glass collection was formed between 1900 and 1910 by the Manchester School of Art. During this decade the school bought English, American, Bohemian and Venetian art glass, of which only a proportion is now extant. Of fifteen Tiffany glasses acquired in 1903 for example, two remain (nos. G15 and G16). However some splendid Powell pieces survive (eg nos. G7 and G8) among a group of about twenty. The glass formed part of general collections of applied art (especially textiles, ceramics and metalwork), representative of design trends in the early years of this century.

North West Collections—the twentieth century

The developments in collecting so noticeable at the turn of the century were to some extent checked by the First World War and the depression which followed. Of the generation of north-west collectors who followed Joseph Mayer, Roscoe died in 1915, Leicester Collier in 1917 and Lloyd Roberts in 1920, while the collections of Jesse Haworth had passed to the Manchester Museum by 1912. Traditions nevertheless were established at this time which collectors of the later part of the century followed as best they could. English eighteenth century glass in particular continued to be sought. Curiously, the collectors were often medical men like Lloyd Roberts. Dr Henry Holroyd of Burnley (d. 1932), a school medical officer, bought mostly drinking glasses from his own neighbourhood (nos. E16 and E17) and Dr H.J. Taylor (d. 1945), an opthalmic surgeon in Preston, acquired a small collection containing some attractive eighteenth century examples (nos. E8 and E9). A distinguished Manchester physician, Professor Frank Tylecote (d. 1965) left some 250 pieces of glass, mostly English eighteenth century, to the Manchester City Art Galleries (no. E36). Inevitably perhaps these collections had not the quality of those assembled earlier by Roscoe and Lloyd Roberts. However one other north-west collection, now split between the Victoria and Albert Museum and several museums and galleries in the Merseyside region, does complement these two fine collections - that of Walter Harding of Birkenhead (1868 - 1936). Formed essentially by 1925, when Harding privately published

a catalogue of his glass, it was notable for its cut glass of the later eighteenth and early nineteenth century (eg no. E57). Harding followed the current enthusiasm for 'Irish' glass, which otherwise found scant favour with north-west collectors.

Little attempt was made after 1920 to extend collections of contemporary and modern glass. Manchester City Art Galleries bought some industrial art glass during the 1930s but the most remarkable accession of recent glass was made by the Oakhill Museum at Accrington. This was the extensive collection of Tiffany glass formed by Joseph Briggs and now in the Haworth Art Gallery. Joseph Briggs (1873 - 1936) had trained in Lancashire as an engraver in a calico printing works. He went to America and joined Louis C. Tiffany in the early 1890s, eventually becoming Art Director in the Tiffany Company. When Tiffany himself withdrew from the declining company in 1920 Briggs had control of all the remaining stock. Exactly how and when Briggs formed his own collection is uncertain but it is representative of more than two decades of Tiffany production (eg nos. G13 and G22). When he returned to Accrington in 1933 Briggs divided his glass between his family and the Accrington Corporation. The public collection of Tiffany glass is the largest and finest in the country.

The development of collections of English glass and art nouveau glass continued trends of the turn of the century. Almost entirely neglected until recent years was the factory glass of the nineteenth century. The sophistication and technical perfection of this glass found few admirers among collectors who responded to the charms of flaws and striations in glass. Museums likewise failed to appreciate the importance of the history of glass in the nineteenth century; not until 1951 did the Stourbridge Council form a collection representative of the great nineteenth century glassmaking traditions of that area. In the north-west the Warrington Museum has steadily acquired specimens of local manufacture (nos. F15 and F20) but Manchester has only within the past few years begun collecting examples of Manchester glass (no. F16), described by the Art Journal in 1851 as 'in no way inferior to the best in the country.'(10) Currently the Pilkington Glass Museum at St Helens is acquiring glass (nos. F2 and F11) to illustrate particularly the technical achievements of the nineteenth century, but in the north-west, as elsewhere, the lack of such glass is unfortunate and will be increasingly expensive to remedy.

Conclusion

The foundation of the Pilkington Glass Museum at St Helens in 1964 gave the north-west the first purpose-built glass museum in the country. A collection of historic glass was quickly established and displayed to illustrate the history of vessel glass, particularly in its technical aspects. A new and distinctive specialisation was thus added to the history of glass collecting in the north-west. The didactic purpose of the Pilkington collection is nevertheless but a modern expression of that spirit which in the past moved men like Joseph Mayer or Jesse Haworth to endow public collections with works of beauty and historical interest.

References

1. The Scriptores Historiae Augustae vol. III. Tacitus XI.3. Loeb Classical Library 1932

2. J.B. Waring. A Handbook to the Museum of Ornamental Art in the Art Treasures Exhibition. London 1857, p.4.

3. J.B. Waring. ibid., p.10.

4. Quoted in G. Reitlinger, The Economics of Taste vol. II. London 1963, p.452.

5. J.B. Waring. ibid., p.7.

6. A. Hartshorne. Old English Glasses. London 1897, p.272 footnote.

7. see W.A. Thorpe 'The Origins of the Circle of Glass Collectors'. The Glass Circle I. London 1972, pp.7-9.

8. see W.A. Thorpe 'The Roscoe Collection of English Glass'. The Connoisseur Oct. 1935, pp.205-209.

9. W.A. Thorpe 'English Glass at the Manchester City Art Gallery'. The Collector Oct. 1930, p.92, fig. 3.

10. The Art Journal Illustrated Catalogue to the Exhibition of the Industry of All Nations, London 1851, p.290.

11. H. Tait 'The Pilkington Museum of Glass I and II'. The Connoisseur Dec. 1964 and Jan. 1965.

The Ancient World

The glass in this part of the catalogue is described under three main periods: Egyptian, Hellenic and Hellenistic, and Roman. The Roman period is further subdivided according to techniques of manufacture and decoration. All the glass is presumed to be of soda-lime type.

EGYPTIAN GLASS

A1
KOHL POT

Dark blue glass, much weathered. Core-formed, with alternate white and yellow trails in a zig-zag pattern on the body; on the neck horizontal relief trails of similar colours beneath nine vertical relief trails, probably all yellow; a white relief trail circles the base.
h. 8.6 cm

The Manchester Museum 5318
Found Gerzeh, Egypt. Acquired by subscription from the British School of Archaeology, Egypt, in about 1910-11.

Egyptian
18th Dynasty: c. 1400 B.C.

A2
ALABASTRON

Royal blue glass. Core-formed, with turquoise
and white horizontal relief trails at the
shoulder and two yellow glass projections on
the body. On the rim are two relief trails, a
yellow and turquoise twisted trail above and
a yellow trail, striped with turquoise, below.
h. 15.7 cm

Merseyside County Museums M11763
Found Egypt. Acquired from the Sams
Collection by Joseph Mayer. Mayer gift, 1867.

Refs: Sams (1839) p46, no 165; Gatty (1879)
p66, no 501a.

Egyptian
18th Dynasty: c. 1400 B.C.

A3
AMPHORISKOS

Dark blue glass. Core-formed, with, on the
body, a turquoise and yellow trail each above
and below trails of white, yellow and
turquoise in feather pattern; on the neck zig-
zag trails in similar colours, with a twisted
black and white cord encircling the rim. The
handles in black glass, with fine inlaid white
and yellow trails. Damaged on side during
manufacture.
h. 8.3 cm

Merseyside County Museums M10157
Mayer gift, 1867.

Egyptian
19th Dynasty: c. 1300 B.C.

A4
FLASK

Dark royal blue glass. Core-formed, flat-sided, one handle missing. On the body, horizontal trails of blue and yellow with yellow trails in feather pattern; blue and yellow zig-zag trails on the neck with a twisted cord of purple and yellow on the rim. The handle is of purple glass with three yellow vertical stripes.
h. 8.7 cm

The Manchester Museum 727
Found Medinet el Gurob, Egypt, in same deposit as A5. Jesse Haworth gift, 1912.

Refs: Petrie (1891) p17, pl XVIII, 19.

Egyptian
19th Dynasty: c. 1300 B.C.

A5
CUP

Translucent amethyst glass. Probably cast, and polished internally; zig-zag trails of white, yellow and pale blue on the body and a twisted cord of dark and white glass around the rim. The loop handle of dark blue glass is edged with yellow glass and has fine trails of yellow and pale blue.
d. 7.5 cm

The Manchester Museum 728
Found Medinet el Gurob, Egypt, in same deposit as A4. Jesse Haworth gift, 1912.

Refs: Petrie (1891) p17, pl XVIII, 18;
Nolte (1968) p74 no 3, pl XVI, 3;

Harden (1969) p52, pl 3, D.

Egyptian
19th Dynasty: c. 1300 B.C.

A6
ALABASTRON

Translucent deep blue glass. Core-formed, with
yellow trails above and below zig-zag trails of
yellow and turquoise; a relief trail of opaque
turquoise circles the rim; the handles are
deep blue.
h. 10 cm

Merseyside County Museums 1977.113.1
Found Rhodes. Acquired from W. Talbot
Ready in 1903 by F.C. Danson; bequeathed
by his son, Col J.R. Danson, 1977.

Hellenic period
C6 - C5 B.C.

A7
ARYBALLOS

Translucent blue glass. Core-formed; opaque
yellow trail on shoulder and upper body,
where it forms a zig-zag pattern above a zig-
zag opaque turquoise trail; below is a mixed
yellow-turquoise trail and a yellow trail; an
opaque turquoise relief trail circles the rim.
The handles are of translucent blue.
h. 6.3 cm

Merseyside County Museums 39.4060.28
Found Egypt. Sir Robert Mond bequest, 193

Hellenic period
C6 - C5 B.C.

A8
AMPHORISKOS

Translucent greyish-blue glass. Core-formed;
opaque yellow horizontal trails on shoulder
and upper and lower body; zig-zag trails of
opaque yellow and turquoise between these.
A relief trail of opaque yellow circles the rim;
the handles are of greyish-blue glass.
h. 7 cm

Merseyside County Museums M 10154
Mayer gift, 1867.

Hellenic period
C6 - C5 B.C.

A9
KOHL TUBE AND STOPPER

Translucent royal blue glass. Rod-formed,
with opaque white trails in a feathered
pattern; two handles in royal blue glass with
lugs beneath. The stopper of dark translucent
blue glass, core-formed, with relief trails of
opaque turquoise, one forming a knob, below
which are traces of a bronze thread.
h. (incl. stopper) 12.7 cm

Merseyside County Museums M10085
Mayer gift, 1867.

Refs: Barag (1975) p29, fig 53.

Hellenic period: perhaps Rhodes
C4 B.C.

A10
ALABASTRON

Translucent dark royal blue glass. Core-
formed, with trails of yellow, white and green
in a feathered pattern on the body; a relief
yellow trail circles the rim. The handles are
of translucent royal blue glass.
h. 14.7 cm

Merseyside County Museums M 10079
Mayer gift, 1867.

Hellenistic period
C4 - C3 B.C.

A11
HYDRIA

Translucent dark blue glass. Core-formed,
with indentations produced as the decoration
was applied; zig-zag trails of yellow and
turquoise on shoulder and body. The handles
are in dark blue glass.
h. 6.5 cm

Merseyside County Museums M 10162
Mayer gift, 1867.

Hellenistic period
C4 - C3 B.C.

A12
PYXIS

Colourless glass with olive green tint. Cast and polished, the rim with a lip for the (missing) lid; a moulded circle underneath the base at its centre.
d. (base) 12.1 cm; d. (rim) 9.5 cm

The Manchester Museum 21013
Sharp Ogden gift, 1936.

Hellenistic period: Cretan group of pyxides C4 - C3 B.C.

A13
CONICAL BOWL

Colourless glass. Cast, then ground and polished inside and out; two thin grooves circle the bowl below the rim on the exterior. Three holes drilled in the Roman period to attach bronze chains, for use as a lamp.
h. 8.5 cm; d. (rim) 13.2 cm

Merseyside County Museums M 10199
Mayer gift, 1867.

Refs: Thorpe (1938) p14, fig 4.

Hellenistic period: perhaps Syrian C2 - C1 B.C.

A14
SMALL BOWL

Millefiore glass. Mould-pressed, with
polychrome sections of canes of concentric
patterns grouped to form an overall honey-
comb pattern; base ring of purple glass.
h. 3.6 cm; d. (rim) 8.9 cm

Merseyside County Museums 1978-141
Bought, 1978.

Roman period: Eastern Mediterranean
C1 A.D.

A15
SMALL DISH

Blue and white marbled glass, mould-pressed.
d. 8 cm

Pilkington Glass Museum, St Helens 1975.1
Bought, 1975.

Roman period: Alexandria
C1 A.D.

A16
PILLAR-MOULDED BOWL

Transparent amber glass with opaque white
marbling. Mould-pressed, ground and
polished inside and on exterior of rim.
Twenty ribs on body below everted rim.
h. 5.5 cm; d. (rim) 10.5 cm

Merseyside County Museums M 10078
Mayer gift, 1867.

Roman period
Mid C1 A.D.

A17
DISH

Colourless glass. Cast and ground, with ring
base.
d. (rim) 10.3 cm; d. (base) 4.6 cm

The Manchester Museum 21004
Sharp Ogden gift, 1936.

Roman period
C2 - C3 A.D.

A18
SQUARE BOTTLE

Deep bluish-green tinted glass. Mould-blown,
with four raised concentric rings on the base.
The rim folded to form a lip inside the neck;
broad strap handle.
h. 31.5 cm

Merseyside County Museums M 10057
Mayer gift, 1867.

Roman period: possibly Rhenish
Late C1 or C2 A.D.

A19
FLASK

Transparent green glass. Mould-blown in the
form of a double-head flask, with a small
animal, possibly a horse, moulded on the
base. Most of the rim restored.
h. 8 cm

Pilkington Glass Museum, St Helens 1970-10
Bought, 1970.

Roman period
C2 - C3 A.D.

A20
FLAT BOTTLE

Transparent greenish blue glass. Mould-blown
in ribbed mould, giving diagonal fluting on the
body; the rim is folded in and the base has a
slight kick.
h. 22.3 cm

Bolton Museum and Art Gallery A.94.1969
Found Syria; bought, 1969.

Roman period: Eastern Mediterranean
(perhaps Egypt)
C2 - C3 A.D.

A21
SHALLOW BOWL

Transparent pale greenish glass. Mould-blown,
slight fluting on the base; the wall of the
vessel is folded to form an exterior ledge
which runs between the two trailed handles;
base with a slight kick.
h. 5.4 cm; d. (rim) 12.8 cm

Bolton Museum and Art Gallery BA4
Details of acquisition unknown.

Roman period: possibly Egypt
C2 - C3 A.D.

A22
BARREL JUG

Colourless, bubbly glass with faint green tint.
Mould-blown with five horizontal corrugations
at the shoulder and seven at the base; the rim
folded in, then flared out and flattened;
applied handle. On the base three moulded
concentric rings surrounded by an inscription,
'CEREL ATTICI', with a heart-shaped leaf
between each word.
h. 18.5 cm

Merseyside County Museums M 10062
Mayer gift, 1867.

Roman period: Gaul
Late C3 A.D.

A23
FLASK

Transparent amber glass. Mould-blown, the
lower body in the form of a bunch of grapes;
concentric rings on base; the rim is folded
out, down and then inwards.
h. 16.5 cm

Pilkington Glass Museum, St Helens 1978-11
Bought, 1978.

Roman period
C3 - C4 A.D.

A24
JUG

Yellowish green glass. Mould-blown with body
pattern of raised bosses; a folded ridge at the
base of the neck and an inturned rim. The
base is pushed in, the handle applied.
h. 13 cm

Merseyside County Museums 28.8.99.2
Found Jaffa; bought from J. McKitterick, 1899.

Roman period: Syria
C3 - C4 A.D.

A25
JUG

Colourless glass with slight greenish tint.
Mould-blown in hexagonal form, with panels
of i) lattice work ii) palm branch iii)
diamonds enclosing circles, repeated once.
Rim folded in and base slightly pushed in;
trail around the neck and handle applied.
h. 13.5 cm

Merseyside County Museums 61.72.15
Probably collected on Mt Carmel by Col
Stanton; from the collection of Mrs Holden.
Presented by her daughter in 1961.

Roman period: Syria
C4 - C5 A.D.

A26
STEMMED CUP

Colourless glass with yellowish tint. Mould-
blown in a ribbed mould, the ribs diagonal
below a ridge circling the body; pad base.
h. 10 cm

The Manchester Museum 20989
Details of acquisition unknown.

Roman period
C4 - C5 A.D.

14

A27
FLASK

Transparent pale blue glass. Mould-blown in
a ribbed mould; blue spirals around the neck
and a thick blue trail on the rim; base slightly
pushed in.
h. 15.8 cm

Bolton Museum and Art Gallery BA9
Details of acquisition unknown.

Roman period: Syria
C4 - C5 A.D.

A28
JAR

Colourless glass with pale green tint,
iridescent. Mould-blown with fine diagonal
ribbing on the body; rim flattened and
thickened. A trail of deep turquoise forms a
coil base and another circles just below the
rim. Two handles of deep turquoise and red
glass.
h. 9 cm

The Manchester Museum 21072
James Shaw gift, 1937.

Roman period
C4 A.D.

A29
BOWL

Clear deep amber glass. Blown, with fourteen
pinched ribs from the shoulder to the base;
the rim is ground and a wheel-ground line
circles the exterior of the neck.
h. 6.8 cm; d. (rim) 8.3 cm

The Manchester Museum 1975.75
Bought, 1975.

Roman period
Mid C1 A.D.

A30
JAR WITH LID (CINERARY URN)

Colourless glass with bluish-green tint. Blown,
the jar with rim folded inwards and the base
pushed in; the bottle-neck lid has a disc
applied to seal the opening. Two M-shaped
handles.
h. (with lid) 35.2 cm; d. (body rim) 17.5 cm

Merseyside County Museums 1977.113.5
Possibly bought in London in 1910 by F.C.
Danson; bequeathed by his son Col J.R.
Danson, 1977.

Roman period: Western Gaul or Italy
Late C1 - early C2 A.D.

A31
JAR WITH LID

Colourless glass with light greenish tint.
Blown, the body folded out, down and in,
and then flattened, the base slightly pushed
in. The bottle neck lid has a similar rim to the
body.
h. (with lid) 27.7 cm; d. (body rim) 16.5 cm

Merseyside County Museums 1977.113.11
Found Ventimiglia, Franco-Italian border;
probably bought c1910 by F.C. Danson;
bequeathed by his son, Col J.R. Danson, 1977.

Roman period: Gaul
Late C1 - early C2 A.D.

A32
DISH

Colourless glass with greenish tint. Blown,
oval shape with rim folded out and down, and
the pad base tooled to form a base ring.
h. 4.8 cm; d. (rim) 22.2 cm x 15.2 cm

The Manchester Museum 20182
Details of acquisition unknown.

Roman period: Egypt
C3 - C4 A.D.

A33
AMPHORISKOS

Transparent purple glass, iridescent. Blown,
with a purple trail just below the rim and two
purple handles.
h. 15 cm.

Merseyside County Museums 1977.113.31
Bequeathed by Col J.R. Danson, 1977.

Roman period: Syria
C3 - C4 A.D.

17

A34
JUG

Transparent yellowish green glass. Blown,
with thickened rim. Beneath the rim a
turquoise and red trail and another forming a
coil base; a fine trail of yellowish green around
the base of the neck. The ribbed strap handle
is of turquoise and red glass.
h. 14.8 cm

The Manchester Museum 20672
Sharp Ogden gift, 1936.

Roman period
C3 - C4 A.D.

A35
AMPHORISKOS

Transparent amber glass. Blown, the rim
folded up and in. A trail of red and turquoise
around the neck and two turquoise glass
handles.
h. 23 cm

The Manchester Museum 20677
Sharp Ogden gift, 1936.

Roman period
C4 A.D.

A36
SMALL BOTTLE

Colourless glass. Blown, with pushed-in base.
A turquoise trail around the neck below the
rim and another lower down; four turquoise
trailed handles, each trail slightly streaked
with red.
h. 7.1 cm

Bolton Museum and Art Gallery A53.1971
Found Tyre, 1899; bought, 1971.

Roman period: Syria
C4 A.D.

A37
JAR

Colourless glass with slight greenish tint,
iridescent. Blown, the neck with a tooled
flange half way down. Zig-zag turquoise trail
on the body, the two handles of colourless
greenish glass touching the neck flange.
h. 8.1 cm

Merseyside County Museums 28.8.99 4
Found Jaffa; bought from J. McKitterick, 1899.

Roman period: Syria
C4 A.D.

A38
JUG

Transparent amber glass. Blown, the rim
turned out and flattened, the base pushed in.
Under the rim a thick amber trail; a ribbed
handle of amber glass.
h. 13 cm

Bolton Museum and Art Gallery A92.1969
Found Syria; bought, 1969

Roman period: Eastern Mediterranean
C4 A.D.

A39
STEMMED JUG

Transparent olive green glass. Blown, with
rim folded over and the stem and base drawn
from the body and slightly ribbed. An olive
green trail under the rim; the strap handle
also olive green.
h. 17.8 cm

The Manchester Museum 20674
Sharp Ogden gift, 1936.

Roman period
C4 A.D.

A40
JAR

Transparent green glass. Blown, the rim
thickened and folded in, the base pushed in;
part of rim missing. A green zig-zag trail runs
twice round vessel from the shoulder to the
middle of the body, forming a series of
lozenges.
h. 14.5 cm

The Manchester Museum 3358
Found Saft el Henneh, Egypt, grave 725;
acquired by subscription from the British
School of Archaeology, Egypt, 1906.

Refs: Petrie (1906) pl XXXVIIIA, 41.

Roman period
C4 A.D.

A41
JAR

Transparent olive green glass, weathered inside.
Blown, with rim folded up and in; base ring.
An olive green trail spirals from under the rim
around the upper part of the neck.
h. 11.9 cm

The Manchester Museum 6162
Found Harageh, Egypt; acquired by
subscription from the British School of
Archaeology, Egypt, 1913-1914.

Roman period
C4 - C5 A.D.

A42
JUG

Pale green glass, iridescent. Blown, the trefoil
mouth with rim folded in; the handle also in
pale green glass.
h. 13.8 cm

The Manchester Museum 20675
Sharp Ogden gift, 1936.

Roman period
C4 - C5 A.D.

A43
QUADRUPLE PERFUME FLASK

Transparent green glass, iridescent within.
Blown in two parts, each pinched to form two
tubes and then fused together, the rims folded
in, the base flattened; a transparent turquoise
trail, now incomplete, winds from near the
base to below the rim.
h. 9.8 cm

Merseyside County Museums 29-3-92-13
Found Nazareth, 1891; bought from T.E.
Tomlinson & Co, 1892.

Roman period: Syria
C4 - C5 A.D.

44
FOUR DOUBLE PERFUME FLASKS

(a)
Transparent green glass. Blown as one tube and pinched to form two, the thickened rim folded in; a fine horizontal green trail and six vertical green trails on the body; single loop handle.
h. (incl. handle) 18.2 cm

Bolton Museum and Art Gallery A.93.1969
Found Syria; bought, 1969.

Roman period: Syria
C4 - C5 A.D.

(b)
Transparent pale olive green glass. Blown as one tube and pinched to form two, the rims folded in, the base flattened; two handles of turquoise glass with threads of red develop to pinched trails running down the sides of the body.
h. 11.2 cm

Merseyside County Museums 29-3-92-11
Found Nazareth, 1891; bought from T.E. Tomlinson & Co, 1892.

Roman period: Syria
C4 - C5 A.D.

(c)
Transparent pale green glass, iridescent. Blown
as one tube and pinched to form two, the rims
folded in; a fine turquoise trail horizontally
around the lower body. The basket handle
is formed from a thick pale green trail.
h. (incl. handle) 16 cm

Merseyside County Museums 29-3-92-12
Found Nazareth, 1891; bought from T.E.
Tomlinson & Co, 1892.

Roman period: Syria
C4 - C5 A.D.

(d)
Transparent bluish green glass. Blown as one
tube and pinched to form two, the rims folded
in; a transparent turquoise trail spirals the
body and two turquoise pinched trails at either
side of the body form handles near the rim.
h. 12 cm

Merseyside County Museums 29-3-98-61
Found Tiberias; bought from G.F. Lawrence,
1898.

Roman period: Syria
C5 A.D.

A45
CUP

Colourless glass. Moulded blank with a
central panel of interlocking wheel-ground
facets; base and body polished on the wheel.
h. 8.5 cm   d. (rim) 10.2 cm

The Manchester Museum 11243
Found Haifa, Israel; Robinow gift, 1959.

Refs: Thorpe (1938) p17, fig 7.

Roman period
Late C1 - early C2 A.D.

A46
FLASK

Colourless glass with faint green tint,
encrusted on much of inner surface. Blown,
with pushed-in base; wheel-ground design of
four trees, each set in a panel bordered by
diagonal hatching and horizontal lines with
lattice work between each panel, band of
ornament around the neck. Rim and
part of neck missing.
h. 10 cm

Merseyside County Museums 28.8.99.19
Found Jaffa; bought from J. McKitterick, 1899.

Roman period: probably Syria
C3 A.D.

A47
STEMMED GOBLET

Colourless glass. Blown, with thickened rim
and trailed collar below; the foot is now
broken. Wheel-ground design of hearts,
commas and elongated lozenges, with borders
of a pair of horizontal lines above and below.
h. 18.5 cm

The Manchester Museum 2082
Found Hawara, Egypt; Jesse Haworth gift,
1912.

Refs: Petrie (1889) p.12, pl XX, 6.

Roman period
C3 A.D.

A48
BEAKER

Slightly opaque white glass. Blown, the rim
tooled inside to form a groove, the foot now
missing; a trail of slightly opaque white below
the rim. Wheel-ground design of a broken
line above a band of herringbone, two further
broken lines, a zone of diamonds and narrow
oval facets, two lines, a band of oval facets
and a broken line. Part of the body ground
smooth.
h. 15 cm

Merseyside County Museums M10200
Mayer gift, 1867.

Refs: Harden (1967-8) p52; Price (1979) fig

Roman period: probably Egypt
C3 - early C4 A.D.

Teutonic glass of the 5th to 7th century A.D. All examples are presumed to be of soda-lime type and are free-blown, unless otherwise stated.

B1
CONE BEAKER

Colourless glass with pale green tint, many tiny bubbles. The rim rounded and thickened, the base missing; fine pale green trails on the upper body, with vertical loops of the same metal, probably a continuous trail, on the lower body. h. approx 22 cm

Merseyside County Museums M6643
Found Ozingell, Kent. Sold c1855 by W.H. Rolfe to Joseph Mayer. Mayer gift, 1867.

Refs: C.R. Smith (n.d.) Vol III, pl iii, 8; D.B. Harden (1956) p159, type III a i.

Frankish: ?Rhineland
C5 - early C6 A.D.

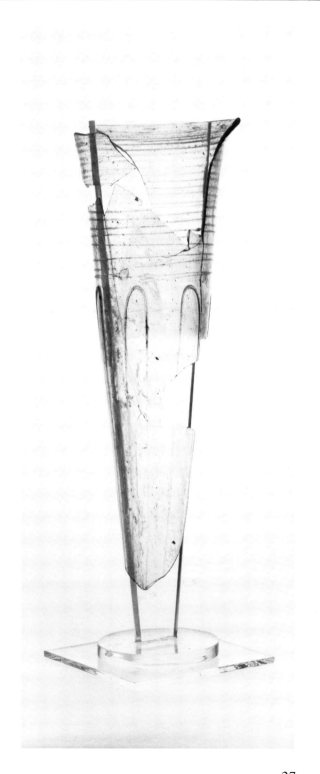

B2
CLAW BEAKER

Transparent dark olive green glass, slightly
bubbly. The upper part of the vessel is
missing; coil base. Olive green trails around
the upper, middle and lower body. There are
two rows of olive green claws, the lower with
three claws pulled down to touch the base,
the upper with two claws surviving, applied
between the middle and upper groups of
trails and pulled down to touch between the
middle and lower trails.
h. (extant) 19 cm

Merseyside County Museums M6073
Found Gilton, Kent, grave 83, outside the
foot of the coffin. Excavated by the Rev. B.
Faussett in 1763; sold in 1854 by the Godfrey
Faussett family to Joseph Mayer. Mayer
gift, 1867.

Refs: C.R. Smith (1856) p27, pl XVIII, fig 2;
D.B. Harden (1956) p159, type IIb.
R. Hurst (1968) p17, pl 17.

Uncertain attribution
Late C5 - early C6 A.D.

B3
TWO PALM CUPS

(a)
Transparent olive green glass, many small bubbles. Rim rounded, with twenty mould-blown ribs rising through the lower part of the body from a circular ridge surrounding the base; within the ridge an equal armed cross having a central boss and a boss in each angle of the cross.
h. 8 cm; d. (rim) 8.5 cm

Merseyside County Museums M6401
Found Kingston Down, Kent, grave 146. Excavated by the Rev. B. Faussett in 1771; sold in 1854 by the Godfrey Faussett family to Joseph Mayer. Mayer gift, 1867.

Refs: C.R. Smith (1856) p69, pl XVIII, fig 4; D.B. Harden (1956) p164, type X a i.

Uncertain attribution
C6 A.D.

(b)
Transparent amber glass, many small bubbles, iridescent, rim rounded. From the same mould as B3a.
h. 8.5 cm; d. (rim) 9 cm

Merseyside County Museums M6513
All other details as for B3a.

Note: glasses are commonly found in pairs in Anglo-Saxon graves. B3a and b both lay to the left of the skull of the skeleton in Kingston grave 146, within the coffin.

B4
BELL BEAKER

Transparent pale olive green glass, tiny
bubbles. Rounded rim; mould-blown ribs run
from a fold above the base to 2 cms below
the rim.
h. 12 cm

Merseyside County Museums M10061
Found Selsen, Germany. Mayer gift, 1867.

Refs: cf D.B. Harden (1956) p161, type Vb.

Frankish
Late C6 - early C7 A.D.

B5
BOWL

Transparent amber glass, some minute and
larger bubbles. Rounded rim; base slightly
pushed in; fine amber trails on the neck and
centre of the body.
h. 7.3 cm; d. (rim) 6.5 cm

Merseyside County Museum M7002
Found Ozingell, Kent. Sold c1855 by W.H.
Rolfe to Joseph Mayer. Mayer gift, 1867.

Refs: C.R. Smith (n.d.) Vol III, pl iii, 6;
D.B. Harden (1956) p164, type VIII a ii.

Anglo Saxon: Kent (?Faversham)
Late C6 - early C7 A.D.

Note: this glass was described by C.R. Smith
(ibid) as of amethyst colour, apparently
before it had been cleaned of iridescence.

B6
BAG BEAKER

Colourless glass with bluish green tint, very bubbly. Rounded and thickened rim; a pinched bluish green trail around the upper body continues upwards as a thin spiralling trail; four trails of similar glass form eight vertical ribs, alternately pinched, on the lower body and across the base.
h. 18.9 cm

Merseyside County Museums M6647
Found Gilton, Kent. Sold c1855 by W.H. Rolfe to Joseph Mayer. Mayer gift, 1867.

Refs: Akerman (1855) p34, pl xvii 2;
D.B. Harden (1956) p163, type VIa;
D.B. Harden (1972) p89, fig 6,6.

Anglo-Saxon: Kent (?Faversham)
C7 A.D.

B7
SQUAT JAR

Transparent bluish green glass, very bubbly. Rounded rim; the base slightly pushed in.
h. 8.6 cm

Merseyside County Museums M6117
Found Kingston Down, Kent, grave 9, at right side of the skull within the coffin. Excavated by the Rev. B. Faussett in 1767, sold in 1854 by the Godfrey Faussett family to Joseph Mayer. Mayer gift, 1867.

Refs: C.R. Smith (1956) p44, pl XIX, fig 6;
D.B. Harden (1956) p164, type VIIIc.

Anglo-Saxon: Kent (?Faversham)
Probably C7 A.D.

B8
POUCH BOTTLE

Transparent green glass, few tiny bubbles.
Trailed rim, flared out then folded in on
itself; green trail from the base zig-zags to
shoulder and down four times, then
apparently continues onto shoulder to
spiral around the neck.
h. 10.8 cm

Merseyside County Museums M6583
Found Barfriston Down, Kent, grave 28, at
foot of child's skeleton. Excavated by the
Rev. B. Faussett in 1772; sold in 1854 by
the Godfrey Faussett family to Joseph
Mayer. Mayer gift, 1867.

Refs: C.R. Smith (1856) p140, pl XVIII, fig 3;
D.B. Harden (1956) p163, type VIIa.

Anglo Saxon: Kent
C7 A.D.

B9
POUCH BOTTLE

Transparent bluish green glass, some small
bubbles. Rounded rim, a bluish green trail
spirals round the neck.
h. 14 cm

Merseyside County Museums M6640
Found Barfriston Down, Kent, grave 48.
Excavated by the Rev. B. Faussett in 1772;
sold in 1854 by the Godfrey Faussett
family to Joseph Mayer. Mayer gift, 1867.

Refs: C.R. Smith (1856) p143, pl XIX, 4;
D.B. Harden (1956) p163, fig 25, type VIIb.

Anglo Saxon: Kent
C7 A.D.

Note: this bottle and a similar one
(Merseyside County Museums M6596) were
found at the feet of the skeleton in grave 48,
Barfriston, within the coffin. The grave also
contained five gold and garnet pendants
dating c625 - 650 A.D.

32

B10
PALM CUP

Transparent bluish green glass with brown tint, many small bubbles. Rim folded out and down in a thick, hollow form; tooled ledge inside.
h. 5.8 cm; d. (rim) 11.8 cm

Merseyside County Museums M6387
Found Sibertswold Down, Kent, grave 7, at the feet of the skeleton within the coffin. Excavated by the Rev. B. Faussett in 1772; sold in 1854 by the Godfrey Faussett family to Joseph Mayer. Mayer gift, 1867.

Refs: C.R. Smith (1856) p104, pl XIX, fig 2; D.B. Harden (1956) p164, type Xb.

Uncertain attribution
C7 A.D.

B11
SQUAT JAR

Transparent amber-brown glass, various bubbles. Rounded rim, mould-blown ribs on the body and pushed in base.
h. 10.5 cm

Merseyside County Museums M6594A
Found Barfriston Down, Kent, grave 34. Excavated by the Rev. B. Faussett in 1772; sold in 1854 by the Godfrey Faussett family to Joseph Mayer. Mayer gift, 1867.

Refs: C.R. Smith (1856) p140, pl XIX 3; D.B. Harden (1956) p164, fig 25, type VIIIb.

Anglo-Saxon: Kent (?Faversham)
C7 A.D.

Note: this glass was found with another squat jar (Merseyside County Museums M6594B) by the feet of the skeleton in grave 34, Barfriston, within the coffin. The grave also contained a gold and garnet pendant dating c625 - 650 A.D.

Islamic and Chinese Glass

C1
FLASK

Transparent yellowish glass, heavily weathered.
Blown; yellowish and dark blue or manganese
trails in elaborate network suggesting the form
of a dromedary.
h. 12 cm

Pilkington Glass Museum, St Helens 1972-13
Bought, 1972.

Islamic period: Syria
C7 - C8 A.D.

C2
THREE MINIATURE FLASKS

(a)
Transparent deep blue glass. Cast as a block,
drilled and polished; on four feet. Cut and
polished decoration on body. The neck has
four wheel-ground, roughly oval facets and
smaller circular facets between, on neck edge.
h. 8 cm

Merseyside County Museums M11764
Found Egypt. Mayer gift, 1867.

Refs: Sams (1839) p47, no 166; Mayer
(1856) p22, no 1357.

Islamic period: Egypt
C9 - C10 A.D.

b)
Colourless glass, iridescent. Cast as a block,
drilled and polished; on four feet. Cut and
polished decoration on body.
h. 6.1 cm

Merseyside County Museums 30.205.2
Probably found Samarra; J. Carlton Stitt
gift, 1930.

Islamic period: Egypt
Probably C9 A.D.

c)
Transparent greenish glass, iridescent. Cast
as a block, drilled and polished; originally
on four feet. Cut and polished decoration
on body.
h. 6.8 cm

Merseyside County Museums 30.205.3
Probably found Samarra; J. Carlton Stitt
gift, 1930.

Islamic period: Egypt
Probably C9 A.D.

C3
BOWL

Yellowish pale green glass. Blown, with seven
rosettes around the body formed by
impressing with a patterned tool.
h. 3 cm; d. (rim) 4.3 cm

The Manchester Museum 7443
Found in the cemetery, Hemamieh, deposit
1685; acquired by subscription from the
British School of Archaeology, Egypt,
1923-1924.

Refs: G. Brunton (1930) pl xlix, 1685,
no 4.

Islamic period: Egypt
C9 - C10 A.D.

35

C4
BOTTLE

Colourless glass. Blown, the junction between body and foot marked by a blue enamelled collar with a ruby glass insert on the interior. Gilt and enamelled in blue, red, white and green. The neck with bands of arabesques; also reserved oval panels with a scroll motif. On the shoulders a broad band enclosing an inscription interlaced with foliate scrolls. Below, further foliate scrolls and a scrolled band at the foot.
h. 28.2 cm

Merseyside County Museums 53.114.448
Bought from Dr P. Nelson, 1953.

Islamic period: Syria
Early C14 A.D.

C5
BOTTLE

Transparent pale blue glass. Mould-blown in a ribbed mould, then free-blown; pushed-in pad base and tooled collar below flared rim.
h. 15.6 cm

The Manchester Museum 20667
Details of acquisition unknown.

Islamic period: probably Persia (?Shiraz)
C18 A.D.

36

C6
BOTTLE

Opaque white glass with blue overlay. Blown,
with cameo cut decoration of chrysanthe-
mums, bamboo and prunus amid rockwork
and a blue band trailed on the rim; on the
body the seal of Ku Yüeh Hsüan with
inscription.
h. 20 cm

Lady Lever Art Gallery, Port Sunlight 827
Bought from Jeffery Whitehead sale by Lord
Leverhulme, 1915.

Refs: R.L. Hobson (1924) pp 102, 107,
pl 81.

China: Peking Imperial Factory
Probably Yung-Chêng period (1723-1735 A.D.)

Note: Ku Yüeh Hsüan was Director of the
Imperial Factory at Peking c1730.

C7
VASE

Opaque polychrome overlay glass. Blown,
with low relief cameo cut decoration; on the
shoulder and body archaic bronze motifs and
lappets, separated from the neck by a band
of dragons in red on a ground of fungus; the
neck and foot with stiff leaves, bands of key-
fret and ju-i heads. On the base a Ch'ien Lung
four character mark incised.
h. 29 cm

Lady Lever Art Gallery, Port Sunlight 826
Bought from S.E. Kennedy sale by Lord
Leverhulme, 1918.

Refs: R.L. Hobson (1924) pp 106-7, pl 82.

China: Peking
Perhaps Ch'ien Lung period (1736-1795 A.D.)

37

VENETIAN AND FAÇON DE VENISE GLASS
i Venetian

Two main groups of glass are described. First is Venetian glass or glass of façon de Venise style, made of soda metal and second, glass of Northern and Central Europe, which is presumed to be of potash metal unless otherwise stated.

D1
BOWL

Colourless glass with slight brownish tint. Folded rim and moulded gadroons on the lower part of the bowl, the ribbed foot folded over at the edge. The upper part of the bowl with a gilt scale pattern outlined with enamel dots in white, blue, red and green between borders of white and blue dots; remnants of gilding on the gadroons.
h. 15.3 cm; d. (rim) 29.5 cm

Merseyside County Museums 10.8.76.1
Bought Messrs Wilson & Son, 1876.

Refs: C.T. Gatty (1883) no 201.

Venice
c1500

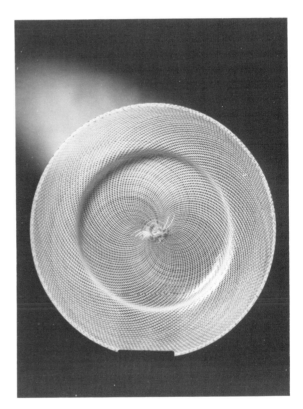

D2
SMALL BOTTLE

Colourless glass with slight greenish tint.
Blown in four-sided mould; colourless trails
along edges, pinched horizontally and
vertically and terminating in prunts; the
neck circled by a blue vermicular collar.
h. 10.1 cm

Pilkington Glass Museum, St Helens 1978.6
Bought, 1978.

Venice
Mid C16 A.D.

D3
PLATE

Colourless glass, with white threads in
'reticello' technique. Rim folded.
d. 22.5 cm

Merseyside County Museums 10.8.76.8
Bought Messrs Wilson & Son, 1876.

Refs: C.T. Gatty (1883) no 217;
R. Hurst (1968) p19, no 9.

Venice
C16 A.D.

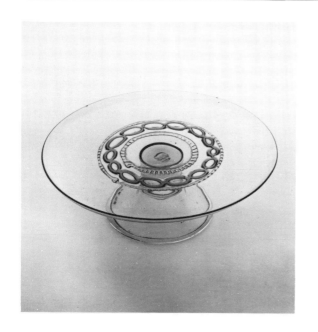

D4
TAZZA

Colourless glass, slightly smoky tint. Rim
curved slightly upwards, the foot with edge
folded over. The centre of the bowl with
two milled trails of colourless glass either
side of a turquoise trailed chain motif;
colourless double thread circuit around the
foot.
h. 6.5 cm; d. (rim) 21 cm.

Merseyside County Museums 11.8.76.4
A.W. Franks gift, 1876.

Refs: C.T. Gatty (1883) no 221.

Probably Venice
c1600

D5
GOBLET

Colourless glass with opaque white glass in
'retorti' technique, the foot with folded edge.
h. 18.8 cm

Merseyside County Museums 11.8.76.1
A.W. Franks gift, 1876.

Refs: C.T. Gatty (1883) no 216; R. Hurst
(1968) p19, no 10.

Venice
Late C16 - early C17 A.D.

40

D6
GOBLET

Colourless glass of grey tint with opaque
white glass in 'retorti' technique; the lower
part of the bowl with mould-blown bosses,
the foot with a plain edge. Most of the upper
bowl and parts of the foot missing.
h. 15.1 cm

**Grosvenor Museum and Art Gallery,
Chester, 652L 1967**
Said to have been found in pieces, during
excavation of the foundations for the
Grosvenor Museum building in 1884/5.

Venice
Late C16 - early C17 A.D.

D7
CUP AND SAUCER

'Calcedonio' glass, brown with blue, green
and purple colouration flecked with
avventurine; the saucer has a deep circular
well to support the cup.
h. (cup) 8.8 cm; d. (saucer) 12.5 cm

Merseyside County Museums 17.8.76.20
Bought from Mr J. McConnell, 1876.

Refs: C.T. Gatty (1883) no 241.

Venice
Late C17 - early C18 A.D.

D8
BELL

Colourless glass with brown tint. Folded rim; five colourless milled trails horizontally, with three lion mask prunts applied over one trail. h. 18.3 cm

Manchester City Art Galleries 1917.678
Leicester Collier bequest, 1917.

Probably Southern Netherlands
Late C16 A.D.

D9
BEAKER

Colourless glass with wrythen opaque white threads; milled foot ring and pushed-in base. On the body three lion mask prunts, gilt, and three vermicular prunts.
h. 16.8 cm; d. (rim) 11 cm

Merseyside County Museums 10.8.76.3
Bought from Messrs Wilson & Son, 1876.

Refs: C.T. Gatty (1883) no 211;
R. Hurst (1968) p20, no 13.

Southern Netherlands: possibly Liège
Late C16 A.D.

D10
COVERED GOBLET

Colourless glass of slight grey tint with opaque white glass in 'retorti' technique; the bowl foot and cover tooled to a stepped shape, the foot rim folded.
h. (with cover) 37.2 cm

Merseyside County Museums 10.8.76.5
Bought from Messrs Wilson & Son, 1876.

Refs: C.T. Gatty (1883) no 213;
R. Hurst (1968) p19, no 11.

Southern Netherlands or Germany
Late C16 - early C17 A.D.

D11
WINEGLASS

Colourless glass.
h. 26.8 cm

Merseyside County Museums 17.8.76.15
Bought from W.C. Rhodes, 1876.

Refs: C.T. Gatty (1883) no 206.

Venice or Netherlands
Late C16 - early C17 A.D.

D12
WINEGLASS

Colourless glass with slight brown tint. The foot folded; the lower bowl with spiked gadrooning below a fine circuit thread; on the stem two opaque yellow glass wings with colourless trails applied and pinched.
h. 12 cm

Merseyside County Museums 17.8.76.13
Bought from W.C. Rhodes, 1876.

Refs: C.T. Gatty (1883) no 205;
R. Hurst (1968) p20, no 14.

Venice or Southern Netherlands
Early C17 A.D.

D13
TAZZA

Colourless glass. The stem with mould-blown wrythen ribs, the foot folded.
h. 15 cm

Merseyside County Museums 11.8.76.5
A.W. Franks gift, 1876.

Refs: C.T. Gatty (1883) no 207.

Probably Netherlands
First half of C17 A.D.

D14
KUTTROLF

Colourless glass of slight grey tint with
opaque white vertical wavy threads; the
foot folded. Opaque white trails on the rim
of the mouthpiece, which terminates the
triple-tubed neck.

h. 22.7 cm

Merseyside County Museums 1.8.78.2
Described as 'received in exchange' from Mr
Wareham, 1878.

Refs: C.T. Gatty (1883) no 210.

Venice or Germany
C17 A.D.

D15
GOBLET

Colourless glass with slight grey tint. The
convoluted stem formed from colourless
incised twist canes with colourless applied
pincered flanges.
h. 21 cm

Merseyside County Museums 10.8.76.6
Bought from Messrs Wilson & Son, 1876.

Refs: C.T. Gatty (1883) no 203.

Netherlands or Germany
C17 A.D.

45

D16
GOBLET

Colourless glass with pinkish-beige tint. The convoluted stem formed from red and opaque white canes with colourless applied flanges.
h. 27.6 cm

Merseyside County Museums 17.8.76.12
Bought from W.C. Rhodes, 1876.

Refs: C.T. Gatty (1883) no 204. .

Netherlands or Germany
C17 A.D.

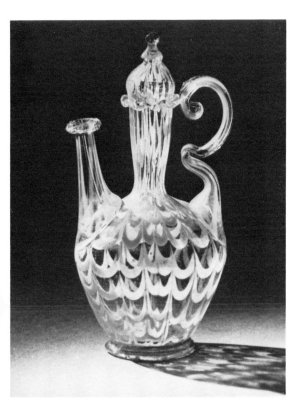

D17
SMALL EWER

Colourless glass with pale yellowish tint. Foot
ring and pushed-in base. Applied colourless
vermicular collar on the neck and applied
colourless rim on the spout; body and neck
with combed opaque white trails.
h. 15.2 cm

Merseyside County Museums 10.8.76.4
Bought Messrs Wilson & Son, 1876.

Refs: C.T. Gatty (1883) no 212;
R. Hurst (1968) p20, no 16.

Spanish: Catalonia
Late C16 - early C17 A.D.

D18
EWER

Colourless glass. Mould-blown in ribbed
mould, the foot formed from a thick trail.
Rim decorated with pincered net pattern and
a trail around the neck; the spout with a
prunt and a trailed lip.
h. 17.8 cm

Williamson Art Gallery, Birkenhead 509.377
John Williamson gift, 1916.

Perhaps Spanish
C17 A.D.

D19
EWER

Transparent yellowish-green glass. The base
deeply pushed in. A trail below the rim and
a pincered lobed trail on the handle.
h. 17.3 cm

Williamson Art Gallery, Birkenhead 508.376
John Williamson gift, 1916.

Perhaps Spanish
Late C17 - early C18 A.D.

D20
SWEETMEAT GLASS

Colourless glass with smoky grey tint. Six
applied colourless pincered flower shapes
on the rim of the bowl, and pincered lobed
trails on the handles; around the stem a
thick colourless collar, with pincered lobes.
h. 10.7 cm

Manchester City Art Galleries 1917-694
Leicester Collier bequest, 1917.

Spanish
C18 A.D.

D21
CUP

Colourless glass, very cloudy. The rim with a
milled trail and the body with pairs of strawberry prunts; foot badly chipped.
h. 2.9 cm

Merseyside County Museums 8130 M
Mayer gift, 1867.

Refs: C.T. Gatty (1883) no 246.

Northern Europe
C14 - C15 A.D.

D22
DAUMENGLAS

Colourless glass. Two rows of finger grips,
three in each row; above and below these two
milled trails. The base edged with a pinched
trail.
h. 19.7 cm

Merseyside County Museums M8118
Mayer gift, 1867

Refs: C.T. Gatty (1883) no 250: 'Vessel
with cover'.

Germany
C17 A.D.

D23
MUG

Colourless glass with greyish tint. Applied
foot with base pushed in. Enamelled; on the
neck the date 1600 in yellow with black
shading and green leaves between the
numerals; blue and green star pattern
opposite the handle; white dots and a
colourless trail, blue splashed, above. On the
body a colourless trail, blue splashed; an
inscription 'DAS WALT GOT D.S.A.S.' in
yellow, blue, white and red between bands
of blue, red and yellow; a green cable
between red bands on lower body with yellow
arcading near foot; below neck a further
green cable.
h. 16.1 cm

Merseyside County Museums 17.8.76.8
Bought Messrs Wilson & Son, 1876.

Refs: C.T. Gatty (1883) no 242.

Bohemia or Southern Netherlands
c1600

D24
BEAKER

Colourless glass. Enamelled in white, blue
and yellow; a crowned double monogram
'F4' within a leaf spray, and the inscription:
'VIVAT REX DANNIAE' all within
horizontal white bands.
h. 9.7 cm

Merseyside County Museums 8120 M
Mayer gift, 1867.

Refs: C.T. Gatty (1883) no 275.

Bohemia or Scandinavia
Early C18 A.D.

Note: the monogram is that of Frederick IV,
King of Denmark from 1699 to 1730.

D25
TANKARD

Translucent white glass. Thin slab handle and tooled base. Rim gilt and gilt sprays either side of handle; enamelled in pale brown, yellow and green; a landscape with river, bridge and figures in a boat framed by columns, scrollwork and a palm tree; two figures overlook the landscape.
h. 16.3 cm

Merseyside County Museums 17.5.75.2 M
J. Sale gift, 1875.

Refs: C.T. Gatty (1883) no 257.

Probably Southern Germany
c1760

D26
MUG

Translucent white glass. Ground rim. Rim gilt and gilt sprays beside handle; enamelled in green, blue, yellow, red, brown and purple; the half-length figure of a huntsman holding a dog on a leash is framed by shell scrollwork amid trees.
h. 8.5 cm

Manchester City Art Galleries 1922.1621
Mrs T.T. Greg gift, 1922.

Bohemia or Germany
c1760

D27
FLASK

Colourless glass. Blown in octagonal
mould. Enamelled in blue, white, red, yellow,
yellowish-green and black; on one side a horse-
man, on three sides vertical flower and leaf
sprays, dot and interlace ornament on the
corners. Metal stopper.
h. 18.5 cm

Williamson Art Gallery, Birkenhead 514
John Williamson bequest, 1916.

Central Europe
C18 A.D.

D28
GOBLET

Colourless glass. Foot pushed in and folded
under to give a hollow rim. Diamond point
engraved, in outline with internal hatching; St
Francis by a tree, with the inscription:
'S Franciscus' beneath and 'F.P.' above,
framed by leafy scrolls; reverse, the infant
Christ between his parents, similarly framed;
between the scrolls a flowered stem.
h. 17.5 cm

Manchester City Art Galleries 1917.689
Leicester Collier bequest, 1917.

Germany
C17 A.D.

D29
GOBLET

Colourless glass. The bowl with moulded and
spiked gadroons, the stem solid, the foot
folded over. Wheel engraved; 'VIVAT'
inscription within fruiting vine.
h. 20.7 cm

Merseyside County Museums 49.18.187
Roscoe bequest, 1949.

Germany or Holland; probably engraved in
Holland.
Late C17 A.D.

D30
COVERED GOBLET

Colourless glass. The stem with hollow knops,
the foot folded under; the cover with hollow
knops. Wheel engraved; continuous landscape, with Perseus and Andromeda and a
port scene; on the foot and cover a circuit
of foliage within borders.
h. 22.2 cm

Pilkington Glass Museum, St Helens 1968/7/8
Bought, 1968.

Southern Germany: Nuremberg
Late C17 A.D.

D31
COVERED GOBLET

Colourless glass. Solid stem and flat foot.
Wheel engraved in intaglio and hochschnitt;
the bowl with eight panels, alternately a
'wild man' beneath a canopy and putti with
fruits and flowers; beneath these are four
female head medallions separated by
acanthus leaves. On the stem a leaf pattern,
the foot with a border of triangular ornament
and a polished star shape cut beneath; on the
lid garlands of fruit and flowers or 'C' scrolls
alternate with lambrequins and acanthus
scrolls or strapwork.
h. (incl. cover) 32.1 cm

Pilkington Glass Museum, St Helens 1971.9
Bought, 1971.

Silesia
c1700

D32
GOBLET

Colourless glass, apparently lead. The twisted stem enclosing a column of air, the foot folded under. Wheel engraved; on the bowl clasped hands holding a flaming heart emerging from clouds within an oval formed by a serpent biting its tail. Inscription 'IAN VAN ALPHEN - MARIA BUITEWEGH ANNO 1703' above a polished ball representing the sun; on the foot three sprays, perhaps originally gilt.
h. 17.6 cm

Manchester City Art Galleries 1966.476
Tylecote bequest, 1966.

Probably Holland: engraved in Holland
c1703

D33
GOBLET

Colourless glass with slight mauve tint. The stem with a tear, the foot folded under. Wheel engraved; band around rim, the bowl with the Royal Arms as borne by British monarchs from 1714-1801, differenced for cadency, bordered by scrolls and sprigs, and set within flags and arms. The base of the bowl with cut flutes and facets; the stem facet cut.
h. 19.5 cm

Merseyside County Museums 49.18.373
Roscoe bequest, 1949.

Germany
c1720-1730

Note: the arms are surmounted by what is apparently intended for the coronet of the Prince of Wales; however there is no inescutcheon in the Hanoverian quarter as normal on his arms at this period. It does not therefore seem possible to identify the arms.

D34
GOBLET

Colourless glass. The stem with a large tear,
the foot ground on the lower edge. Wheel
engraved and gilt; rim gilt, formal leaf and
scrollwork on the bowl, partly gilt; gilt bands
on the stem. The foot with gilt and engraved
floral strapwork.
h. 18.5 cm

Merseyside County Museums 49.18.67
Roscoe bequest, 1949.

Bohemia or Germany
c1720-1740

D35
GOBLET

Colourless glass. Cut and wheel engraved. On
the bowl, within a scrolled cartouche and
beneath a crown, the Royal Arms as borne by
British monarchs from 1714-1801 and a
German coat of arms supported by a seated
lion and the figure of a 'Wildman'. Beneath,
the motto 'DIEU ET MON DROIT', and
behind, a floral chain. Below the rim a
simple fruiting scroll within bands; the base
of the bowl circled by leaf shapes. The stem
cut with short flutes in the centre and on
the edge, and engraved with a circle of laurel.
h. 24.1 cm

Abbot Hall, Kendal 333/63
Anonymous gift, 1963.

Uncertain attribution: cut and engraved in
Germany
C18 A.D.

D36
GOBLET

Colourless glass. The bowl with a solid base
enclosing a tear, the stem teared, the foot
folded under. Wheel engraved; arms of
William IV, Prince of Orange, set within flags
and arms, all above a leaf spray.
h. 23.3 cm

Merseyside County Museums 49.18.185
Roscoe bequest, 1949.

Holland
1740

D37
GOBLET

Colourless glass. The bowl with solid base,
the stem teared, the foot a repair attached
by a glass bit. Wheel engraved; ship framed
by floral scrollwork with baskets of
flowers; inscribed 'HET WELVAREN VAN
HOLLAND'.
h. 22.4 cm

Merseyside County Museums 49.18.186
Roscoe bequest, 1949.

Holland
c1750-1760

D38
WINEGLASS

Colourless glass, with flat foot. Gilt rim, the bowl wheel engraved with the arms of Stanhope and motto 'A DEO ET REGE', framed by shell and scrollwork and leaf sprays; to either side seascapes, supported by scrollwork. Lower bowl with cut flutes, the stem flute and facet cut.
h. 12.9 cm

Manchester City Art Galleries 1920.991
Lloyd Roberts bequest, 1920.

Bohemia
c1760

D39
FOUR WINEGLASSES

Colourless glass, lead, opaque twist stems. Wheel engraved and gilt; two monograms beneath coronets, 'RH' and 'RC 1792', the letters with a leaf spray; bead and reel ornament on rim.
h. (approx) 15.1 cm

Merseyside County Museums 49.18.46
Roscoe bequest, 1949.

Norway
Late C18 A.D.

D40
GOBLET

Colourless glass, with mauve tint. The upper knop of the stem teared, the lower stem hollow. Cut and wheel engraved; running floral scroll engraved on the bowl with cut balls on the rim and cut arcading and flutes on the lower bowl. The stem facet cut, the foot with cut arcades and facets and engraved floral sprigs and dogstooth ornament.
h. 25.5 cm

Merseyside County Museums 49.18.184
Roscoe bequest, 1949.

Germany or Bohemia
c1770-1780

D41
COVERED OVAL BOWL

Colourless glass, bubbly. The base of the bowl ground flat. Cut and gilt, the bowl cut with two rows of flat flutes and a zig-zag motif along the rim; the lower bowl gilt with garlands of flowers and festoons of dots below a frieze of star and circle ornament; gilt lozenges formed of dots and sprigs run across the cut zig-zag motif on the rim. The cover cut with lozenges and flutes and gilt in the manner of the body.
h. (incl cover) 23.6 cm; d. (max) 25.5 cm

Merseyside County Museums M 8114
Mayer gift, 1867.
Refs: C.T. Gatty (1883) no 254.

Probably Bohemia

c1775

High quality table glass in England was of soda-lime type until the development of lead crystal glass by George Ravenscroft in the years 1675 - 1677. All glass described here is lead crystal unless otherwise stated. The divisions of the sections are:

i)   Glass from c1660 - c1685 (soda and early lead glass);
ii) lead glass c1690 - c1750;
iii) engraved glass;
iv) colour twist stems c1760 - 1775;
v)   opaque white glass;
vi) cut glass, English and Anglo-Irish, and Irish glass.

ENGLISH GLASS
i) c1660 - c1685

E1
SMALL DECANTER

Colourless soda glass with brownish tint. The body with 'nipt diamond waies' decoration, a vermicular collar on the neck, the foot folded; hollow handle.
h. 20 cm

Pilkington Glass Museum, St Helens 1966/8
Bought, 1966.

Refs: Pilkington Glass Museum 'Old Catalogue' (n.d.) no 167.

England
c1665

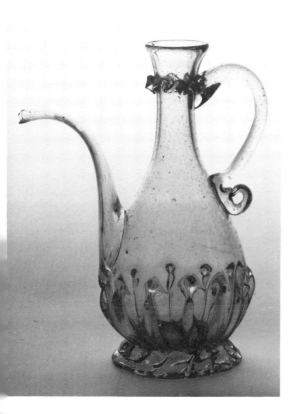

E2
SMALL EWER

Colourless soda glass with greyish tint. The lower body with spiked gadrooning, a vermicular collar on the neck, the foot gadrooned and the base pushed in.
h. 16 cm

Merseyside County Museums M8123
Mayer gift, 1867.

Refs: C.T. Gatty (1883) no 255.

Possibly England, or Netherlands
1650 - 1675

E3
SMALL DECANTER JUG

Colourless glass. The lower body with moulded wrythen gadrooning, a vermicular collar on base of the neck, the rim tooled; the handle has pinched ornament. Stopper with tooled 'pie crust' edge.
h. 13 cm

**Pilkington Glass Museum, St Helens
1963/110/1-2**
Bought, 1963.

Refs: Pilkington Glass Museum 'Old Catalogue' (n.d.) no 174.

England
c1685

E4
ROEMER

Colourless glass. The lower bowl with heavy
moulded gadrooning; the stem hollow with
six circular strawberry prunts.
h. 24.6 cm

Merseyside County Museums 49.18.138
Roscoe bequest, 1949.

Refs: W.A. Thorpe (1929) pl XXXIX.2;
W.A. Thorpe (1935) fig 1b.

England
c1690

E5
TWO BALUSTER WINEGLASSES

(a)
Colourless glass. The bowl with solid base,
stem with wide angular knop over base knop
enclosing an extended tear; the foot folded.
h. 21.5 cm

Merseyside County Museums 49.18.152
Roscoe bequest, 1949.

England
c1700

(b)
Colourless glass. The bowl with solid teared
base, stem with large ball knop between
flattened knops and a base knop; the foot
folded.
h. 17.5 cm

Merseyside County Museums 49.18.140
Roscoe bequest, 1949.

England
c1700

E6
GIANT GOBLET

Colourless glass with slight green/grey tint.
The stem is an inverted baluster with base
knop and large tear throughout, the foot
folded. On the foot an inscription in diamond
point, 'Young Ruler', probably added later.
h. 27.5 cm

Merseyside County Museums 49.18.139
Roscoe bequest, 1949.

England
c1700

E7
WINEGLASS

Colourless glass with slight greenish tint. The
bowl with solid base, stem with cushion knop
above a drop knop, above a teared baluster
with base knop; the foot folded.
h. 17.3 cm

**Harris Museum and Art Gallery, Preston
DRT 103**
H.J. Taylor collection, gift 1945/6.

England
1700 - 1710

E8
WINEGLASS

Colourless glass. The bowl with solid teared
base, stem with annulate teared knop between
two plain columnar sections and base knop;
the foot folded.
h. 18.8 cm

**Harris Museum and Art Gallery, Preston
DRT 102**
H.J. Taylor collection, gift 1945/6.

England
c1710

E9
WINEGLASS OR CORDIAL

Colourless glass. The stem a four-sided
moulded pedestal with elongated tear; the
foot folded.
h. 16.7 cm

**Harris Museum and Art Gallery, Preston
DRT 108**
H.J. Taylor collection, gift 1945/6.

England
1715 - 1720

E10
WINEGLASS

Colourless glass. The bowl with solid base, stem an hexagonal moulded pedestal with elongated tear; the foot folded.
h. 20.6 cm

Harris Museum and Art Gallery, Preston
DRT 64
H.J. Taylor collection, gift 1945/6.

England
c1720

E11
CANDLESTICK

Colourless glass. The socket with moulded ribs and no flange; stem with beaded cushion knop above an octagonal moulded section, diamond-studded at the shoulder, collared at the base and resting on another beaded knop; the foot ribbed and diamond-studded.
h. 24 cm

Merseyside County Museums 49.18.42
Roscoe bequest, 1949.

England
c1745

E12
BOWL AND COVER

Colourless glass. The bowl with moulded
vertical ribs, the cover similarly ribbed with a
wrythen ribbed knop.
h. 23.3 cm

Manchester City Art Galleries 1920.1006
Lloyd Roberts bequest, 1920.

England
c1700 - 1725

E13
SWEETMEAT BOWL AND COVER

Colourless glass. The bowl with trailed and
pincered band and a band of chain decoration.
the cover with two concentric pincered
scalloped bands; finial in the form of a swan.
h. 16.3 cm

Manchester City Art Galleries 1920.1004
Lloyd Roberts bequest, 1920.

England
c1700 - 1725

E14
TWO WINEGLASSES

(a)
Colourless glass. The drawn stem with a tear; the foot folded.
h. 21 cm

Merseyside County Museums 49.18.338
Roscoe bequest, 1949.

England
c1720 - 1740

(b)
Colourless glass. The drawn stem with a tear; the foot folded.
h. 15.5 cm

Merseyside County Museums 49.18.306
Roscoe bequest, 1949.

England
c1720 - 1740

E15
'MEAD' GLASS

Colourless glass. The lower bowl with moulded gadrooning, stem hollow.
h. 15.2 cm

Merseyside County Museums 49.18.158
Roscoe bequest, 1949.

England
Early C18

E16
SWEETMEAT GLASS

Colourless glass. The bowl honeycomb-
moulded, stem with teared cushion knop
above moulded pedestal section with diamond-
studded shoulder above a triple-ribbed collar;
the foot honeycomb-moulded.
h. 14.8 cm

**Towneley Hall Museum and Art Gallery,
Burnley, Holroyd Coll. No 4**
Dr H. Holroyd collection; bequeathed by his
widow, 1935.

England
c1730

E17
SWEETMEAT GLASS

Colourless glass. The bowl with moulded
vertical ribs, stem an incised twist with
central knop; the foot ribbed.
h. 14.7 cm

**Towneley Hall Museum and Art Gallery,
Burnley, Holroyd Coll. No 6**
Dr H. Holroyd collection; bequeathed by his
widow, 1935.

England
c1740

68

E18
CREAM PAIL AND LADLE

Colourless glass. The bowl with folded rim; the junction of handle and bowl marked at either side by a strawberry prunt. Handle surmounted by the figure of a bird.
h. 15.2 cm

Manchester City Art Galleries 1920.1003
Lloyd Roberts bequest, 1920.

Refs: 'Glass in the Manchester City Art Galleries' (1959) no 10.

England
c1700 - 1750

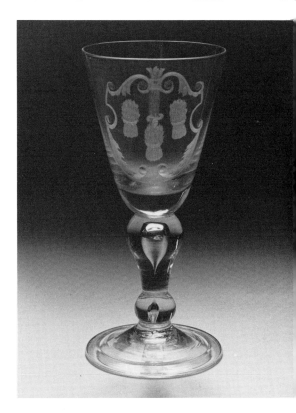

E19
GOBLET

Colourless glass. The stem an inverted
baluster with elongated tear and base knop.
Wheel-engraved; on the bowl the infant
Bacchus astride a barrel, holding a bottle and
a glass, surrounded by fruiting vines; reverse,
a fountain with an oval pool within an
hexagonal grass plot. Below the rim a border
of fruiting vines.
h. 33.3 cm

Manchester City Art Galleries 1920.803
Lloyd Roberts bequest, 1920.

Refs: W.A. Thorpe (1930) fig 2.

England
c1700 - 1710.

E20
WINEGLASS

Colourless glass. The stem an inverted
baluster with tear above teared base knop; the
foot folded. Wheel-engraved; on the bowl the
coat of arms of the City of Chester within a
scrolled shield-shape cartouche.
h. 18 cm

**Grosvenor Museum and Art Gallery,
Chester 95.L.78**
Bought, 1978.

England
c1710 - 1720

E21
TUMBLER

Colourless glass. Wheel-engraved, the arms of Legh and Benet, conjoint, surrounded by scrolling foliage, with the motto 'EN DIEU EST MA FOI' on a ribbon below; reverse, a ram's head out of a ducal coronet.
h. 9.8 cm

Lyme Park; on loan from the Lord Newton Legh family glass.

England
probably 1737

Note: one of a pair of tumblers, probably commemorating the marriage in 1737 of Peter Legh of Lyme (1706-1792) and Martha Benet of Salthrop, Wilts. The ram's head is the Legh crest.

E22
WINEGLASS

Colourless glass. The stem a multi-knop 'Newcastle' baluster, the central ball knop with tears. Diamond-point engraved; on the bowl two badges beneath a coronet, surrounded by foliate and flowered scrolls.
h. 18.9 cm

Merseyside County Museums 49.18.208 Roscoe bequest, 1949.

England: possibly Newcastle
c1745

E23
SWEETMEAT GLASS

Colourless glass. The bowl with sides pressed
in to form an oval at the rim, stem with
central acorn knop between two knops.
Wheel-engraved; on the bowl a baroque
border of scrolls and festoons, partly
polished.
h. 17 cm

Merseyside County Museums 49.18.240
Roscoe bequest, 1949.

Refs: W.A. Thorpe (1929) pl XCIV, 2

England
c1710 - 1720

E24
WINEGLASS

Colourless glass. The drawn stem with a
tear. Wheel-engraved; on the bowl a
baroque border of scrolls and leaf sprays.
h. 20 cm

Merseyside County Museums 49.18.34
Roscoe bequest, 1949.

England
c1720: the engraving possibly later.

E25
WINEGLASS

Colourless glass. The stem a 'Newcastle'
baluster with flattened knop above a beaded
knop, then a plain section above a base knop.
Wheel-engraved; on the bowl a baroque
border of scrolls alternating with stylized
baskets of flowers, highlighted with polished
balls.
h. 18.5 cm

Merseyside County Museums 49.18.207
Roscoe bequest, 1949.

Refs: W.A. Thorpe (1935) fig 1f.

England: possibly Newcastle
c1750

E26
GOBLET

Colourless glass. The stem straight. Cut and
wheel-engraved; on the bowl an engraved
baroque border of formal flowers and foliage
linked by scrollwork; the lower bowl cut in
terraces with a border of sprigs, the stem cut
with alternate flutes and oval slices.
h. 19.5 cm

Merseyside County Museums 49.18.188
Roscoe bequest, 1949.

England
c1750 - 1760

73

E27
WINEGLASS

Colourless glass. The stem a multi-knopped balustroid; the foot folded. Wheel-engraved; on the bowl a prancing horse (the white horse of Hanover) between berried shrubs; above, in diamond point, the inscription 'AUREA LIBERTAS', the central stroke of each letter 'E' missing.
h. 17.1 cm

Manchester City Art Galleries 1920.990
Lloyd Roberts bequest, 1920.

England
c1740 - 1750

E28
WINEGLASS

Colourless glass. The drawn stem with a single cable air-twist. Wheel-engraved; on the bowl a portrait bust of Prince Charles Edward Stuart to sinister, the Garter sash over his right shoulder, within a wreath of crossed laurel branches; reverse, a six-petalled rose with two buds, a thistle spray and bud, and a star.
h. 15.4 cm

Manchester City Art Galleries 1920.905
Lloyd Roberts bequest, 1920; from the Lord Lambourne collection.

England
c1750

74

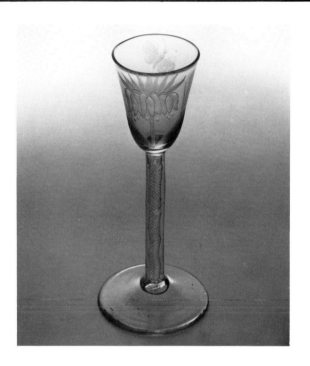

E29
WINEGLASS

Colourless glass. The stem double-knopped
with a multiple spiral air-twist. Wheel-
engraved; on the bowl a spray of apples
and two butterflies.
h. 22.3 cm

Merseyside County Museums 49.18.117
Roscoe bequest, 1949.

Refs: W.A. Thorpe (1935) fig 2b.

England
c1750

Note: the decoration may be derived from
a peach branch on Ch'ien lung porcelain.

E30
WINEGLASS

Colourless glass. The stem a multi-ply air-
twist. Wheel-engraved; on the bowl a Crown
Imperial Lily *(Fritillaria imperialis)* and a
butterfly.
h. 15.8 cm

Manchester City Art Galleries 1920.844
Lloyd Roberts bequest, 1920.

England
c1760

Note: the Crown Imperial Lily was
illustrated by C. de L'Escluse in Rariorum
Plantarum Historia, Vol I. 1601 and
subsequently in several 18th century
botanical works. However, the name,
Fritillaria imperialis, was not used until
published by C. Linnaeus in Species
Plantarum in 1753.

E31
WINEGLASS

Colourless glass. The stem a multi-spiral air-
twist with central swelling. Wheel-engraved;
on the upper bowl a floral and foliate wreath
of passion flower, honeysuckle, poppy and
carnation, with sprays of fruiting vine
between.
h. 16 cm

Merseyside County Museums 49.18.120
Roscoe bequest, 1949.

England
c1750 - 1760

E32
GOBLET

Colourless glass. The drawn stem is straight.
Wheel-engraved; on the bowl a hunt in full
cry pursuing a hare; reverse, an inscription
'Mr Booth and his Little Hounds', within an
oval frame of flowers including honeysuckle,
rose, forget-me-not and poppy.
h. 19.6 cm

Rochdale Museum 2111
Acquired by transfer from Middleton Library
collection, 1974.

England: possibly South Lancashire
c1765 - 1775

E33
GOBLET

Colourless glass, the stem with a central knop. Cut and wheel-engraved; on the bowl an engraved chinoiserie landscape with pavilion; the lower bowl with arch and sprig cutting. The stem is cut with flutes and notches, the knop with relief diamonds.
h. 20 cm

Merseyside County Museums 49.18.190
Roscoe bequest, 1949.

England
c1775

E34
SET OF TWELVE WINEGLASSES

Colourless glass, the stems straight. Cut and wheel-engraved; on the bowls chinoiserie landscapes and figures, rendered differently on each glass; the lower bowls cut in a scale pattern, the stems cut in small concave diamonds.
h. approx 13 cm

Merseyside County Museums 49.18.36 1-12
Roscoe bequest, 1949.

Refs: W.A. Thorpe (1929) pl CXXI;
W.A. Thorpe (1935) pl 6; Victoria and Albert Museum, Catalogue to the Exhibition of English Glass 1968, no 180.

England
c1760 - 1770

E35
TANKARD

Colourless glass. The lower body with
moulded gadrooning and a trail around
the rim; a cavity between the base of the
bowl and the foot contains a shilling of
George II, 1750; strap handle. Wheel-
engraved; on the body the monogram
S.H.M. with an ear of barley to left and
a spray of hops to right.
h. 20.1 cm

Lady Lever Art Gallery, Port Sunlight LG1
W. Harding bequest, 1936.

Refs: Harding (1925) no 56.

England
c1750 - 1760; the engraving probably
added later.

E36
ALE JUG

Colourless glass. Wheel-engraved; on the body
ears of barley and sprays of hops tied with a
bow above the monogram W.S.G; below, a
masonic symbol (divider and set square) and
a small foliate wreath; around the neck foliate
motifs.
h. 15 cm

Manchester City Art Galleries 1966.437
F.E. Tylecote bequest, 1966.

England
Late C18

E37
TANKARD

Colourless glass. The base a tooled flange; plain handle. Wheel-engraved; on the body an oval cartouche with the monogram E.P., surrounded by sprays of mimosa and jasmine; near the handle barley and hops and, below the rim, a wreath of roses.
h. 16 cm

Merseyside County Museums 49.18.229
Roscoe bequest, 1949.

England
Early C19

E38
WINEGLASS COOLER

Colourless glass. Two tooled lips. Cut and wheel-engraved; the lower bowl with cut flutes, an engraved inscription 'LONG LIFE TO THE HOUSE OF LIME' (sic) above, within a curved band.
h. 10.3 cm

Lyme Park; on loan from the Lord Newton
Legh family glass.

England
Early C19

E39
STIRRUP CUP

Colourless glass. Cut and wheel-engraved; on the lower bowl cut flutes below an engraved inscription within an undulating band; 'MAY NONE BUT NINCUMPOOPS KNOW A DRY BOB'; the stem faceted, with faceted knop finial.
h. 13 cm

Lyme Park; on loan from the Lord Newton
Legh family glass.

England
Early C19

Note: this is one of a set of six glasses, each with a different inscription:

'THE AGREABLE (sic) UPS AND DOWNS
 OF LIFE'

'LONG LIFE TO THE HOUSE OF LIME' (Sic)

'MAY ARISTOCRACY RISE ON THE ASHES
 OF DEMOCRACY'

'ANY TOAST BUT A DRY ONE' and

'MRS LEGH'S DELIGHT'

E40
LARGE GOBLET

Colourless glass. The stem straight with flattened knop below the bowl. Wheel-engraved; on the bowl a dove with an oak spray in its beak above foliate sprays and the inscription 'SUCCESS TO THE ROYAL MANCHESTER AND SALFORD VOLUNTEERS'; reverse, an elaborately festooned monogram J.M.H. with the date 1805 below and flower sprays on either side; below the rim a narrow formal border.
h. 30.5 cm

Salford Museum and Art Gallery 18.1940
F. Bindloss gift, 1940.

England: possibly South Lancashire
1805

Note: the the monogram is of Joseph Hanson who was prominent in raising the Manchester Volunteers in 1803.

E41
RUMMER

Colourless glass. The stem with flattened
central knop and collars above and below.
Wheel-engraved; on the bowl H.M.S.
Victory with sails set and gun ports open;
reverse, the inscription 'In Memory of Lord
Nelson Octr 21 1805' within a laurel wreath.
h. 15.1 cm

Manchester City Art Galleries 1920.957
Lloyd Roberts bequest, 1920.

Refs: 'Glass in the Manchester City Art
Galleries' 1959 no 19.

England
1805 or shortly after

E42
RUMMER

Colourless glass. The stem with rounded
knop. Wheel-engraved; on the bowl Nelson's
funeral car, with the coffin under a plumed
canopy inscribed 'TRAFALGAR'; reverse,
the inscription 'LORD NELSON JANY 9
1806' within a laurel wreath.
h. 16 cm

Manchester City Art Galleries 1920.958
Lloyd Roberts bequest, 1920.

England
1806

E43
PAIR OF TUMBLERS

Colourless glass. Wheel-engraved; on the bowl
an oval cartouche with the monogram 'R.M.C.'
surrounded by star-like rays; reverse, a floral
spray with the date '1816' at its base, a bird
in flight to either side; below the rim a band
of formal foliate motifs. The base star cut.
h. 11.3 cm

Manchester City Art Galleries 1920.968
Lloyd Roberts bequest, 1920.

England
1816

E44
RUMMER

Colourless glass. The stem a short pedestal
with square moulded 'lemon squeezer' base.
Wheel-engraved; on the bowl a gentleman's
coach with two pairs of horses; reverse,
the monogram 'WP' within a circle
surmounted by a basket of flowers, with
looped swags of foliage at either side.
h. 19.6 cm

Lady Lever Art Gallery, Port Sunlight LG13
W. Harding bequest, 1936.

Refs: Harding (1925) p58.B.

England
c1830

82

E45
CLARET JUG

Colourless glass. Cut and wheel-engraved; the body with six flute-cut panels, each containing an engraved floral or foliage spray; on the shoulder formal floral motifs. The neck is cut in prismatic rings, the six-sided stopper with formal floral motifs and cut star on top; the base of the body star cut. h. (with stopper) 32.5 cm

Lyme Park; on loan from the Lord Newton Legh family glass.

England
c1830 - 1840

E46
TUMBLER

Colourless glass. Wheel-engraved; on either side of the bowl a semi-circular wreath of oak leaves enclosing the inscription 'ARTILLERY MESS', on one side surmounted by an elephant crest with the inscription 'JAVA', on the other by a sphinx crest with the inscription 'EGYPT'; below the rim a wreath of oak leaves. The base star cut. h. 10.6 cm

Manchester City Art Galleries 1920.974
Lloyd Roberts bequest, 1920.

England
c1830 - 1840

E47
PAIR OF WINEGLASSES

Colourless glass. The stems with central
sapphire blue twisted ribbon encircled by a
double opaque white corkscrew edged with
blue.
h. 18.3 cm

Manchester City Art Galleries 1920.912
Lloyd Roberts bequest, 1920.

Refs: Glass in the Manchester City Art
Galleries (1959) no 16.

England
c1760 - 1770

E48
WINEGLASS

Colourless glass. The stem with a central
opaque white corkscrew edged with red and
green and surrounded by narrow opaque
white threads.
h. 14.6 cm

Manchester City Art Galleries 1920.915
Lloyd Roberts bequest, 1920.

England
c1760 - 1770

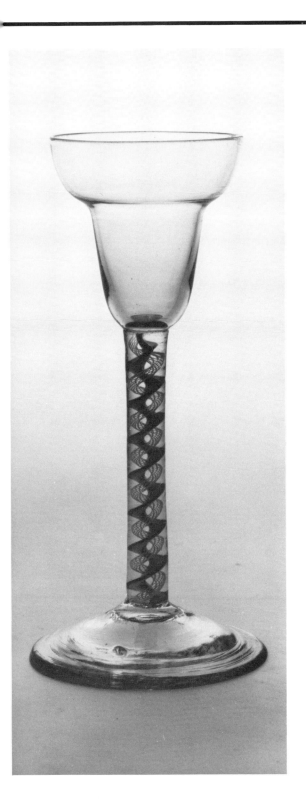

E49
WINEGLASS

Colourless glass. The stem with a central
opaque white corkscrew edged with red and
green, intertwined with a cable of fine
opaque white threads.
h. 14.5 cm

Merseyside County Museums 8127 M
Mayer gift, 1867.

Refs: C T. Gatty (1883) no 247.

England
c1760 - 1770

E50
VASE

Opaque white glass. Enamelled in blue,
green, yellow, pink, brown and rust-red; on
the body Kakiemon style quails under a tree,
and a spray of blossom.
h. 14.2 cm

Merseyside County Museums 49.18.378
Roscoe bequest, 1949.

Refs: W.A. Thorpe (1935) fig 3.

England: probably South Staffordshire
c1760

E51
PAIR OF MINIATURE BOTTLES

Opaque white glass. Enamelled in blue, pink,
puce, green, yellow, brown and iron red; on
the body a seated Chinaman holding a
parasol conversing with a Chinese lady
holding a child on her arm, rockwork and a
tree in the background; reverse, a
conventional spray of flowers in 'famille
rose' manner.
h. 10.5 cm; 11 cm

Merseyside County Museums 16.9.75 4/5
By exchange, from William Edkins, Bristol,
1875; label on base of larger bottle of the
National Exhibition of Works of Art,
Leeds, 1868 no 36.

Refs: C.T. Gatty (1883) no 293.

England: possibly South Staffordshire
c1760

E52
**GARNITURE OF THREE VASES
(CENTRE VASE AND TWO SIDE VASES)**

Opaque white glass. Centre vase with cover.
Oil-gilt; on the body sprays of flowering
foliage, inhabited by an exotic bird, with a
butterfly above; on the centre vase cover are
festoon borders.
h. 24.2 cm; 15.2 cm

Merseyside County Museums 16.9.75 1,2,3
By exchange from William Edkins, Bristol,
1875.

Refs: C.T. Gatty (1883) no 292.

England: possibly London or South
Staffordshire
c1765

E53
SWEETMEAT GLASS

Colourless glass with slight greenish tint. The stem straight. Cut; the bowl with relief diamonds and slices, the rim with arch and angle scallops; the stem faceted hexagonally, the domed foot with lozenges and arch and angle scalloped at the edge.
h. 17.7 cm

Lyme Park; on loan from the Lord Newton
Legh family glass.

England
c1760 - 1770

E54
CREAM JUG

Colourless glass. Cut; the body with alternate vertical flutes and notches, the rim scalloped. The handle is notched and the base star cut.
h. 8.8 cm

Merseyside County Museums 36.137.26
W. Harding bequest, 1936.

Refs. Harding (1925) no 70.

England or Ireland
c1780 - 1800

88

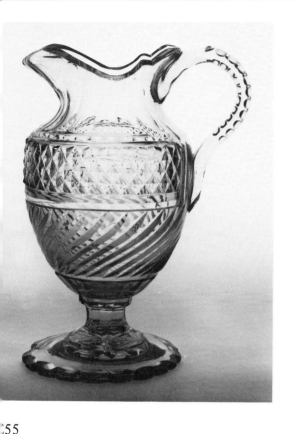

E55
JUG OR EWER

Colourless glass. Cut; the upper body with a horizontal band of small relief diamonds, the lower body with a wide band of slanting blazes; on the neck, the base of the body and the stem are broad flutes. The handle is notched and the foot star cut with a scalloped edge.
h. 27 cm

Merseyside County Museums 36.137.24
W. Harding bequest, 1936.

Refs: Harding (1925) no 120.

Ireland
1800 - 1810

E56
BOAT-SHAPED BOWL AND STAND

Colourless glass. The bowl with oval projection on base to fit stand. Cut; the bowl with a band of lozenges below a band of shallow stars, the rim with arch and angle scallops; the stand cut to match with lozenge borders above and below a band of shallow stars and a scale pattern.
h. 27.5 cm

Merseyside County Museums 1978.374.3
W. Harding bequest, 1936.

Refs: Harding (1925) no 60.

Ireland
Late C18

89

E57
BOAT-SHAPED BOWL AND STAND

Colourless glass. The bowl with oval
projection on base to fit stand. Cut; the bowl
with a horizontal band of slanting lunar slices
between leaflets, the rim with small pointed
scallops and the base star cut; on the stand a
double row of horizontal shallow lozenges,
the upper edge with a similar vertical row and
the base with a band of slanting blazes
between leaflets.
h. 31.5 cm

Williamson Art Gallery, Birkenhead 2284
W. Harding bequest, 1936.

Refs: Harding (1925) no 65.

Ireland
Late C18

E58
BOAT-SHAPED BOWL

Colourless glass with smoky tint. The bobbin
stem rests on a moulded oval foot with radial
lobes. Cut; the bowl with a wide band of
shallow diamonds interspersed with leaflets,
the rim scalloped, with slanting blazes, and
the base with shallow flutes and semicircular
prismatic rings.
h. 24.2 cm

Lady Lever Art Gallery, Port Sunlight LG2
W. Harding bequest, 1936.

Refs: Harding (1925) no 66.

Ireland
c1790

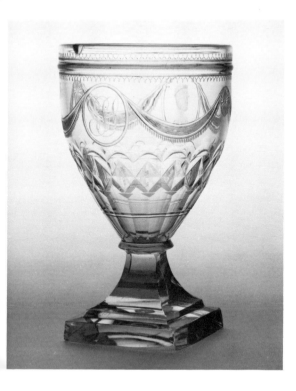

E59
PAIR OF GOBLETS

Colourless glass. The stem a four-sided
pedestal below a collar, the square base solid.
A trail of green glass applied just below the
rim. Cut and wheel-engraved; on the upper
bowl an engraved zig-zag border above and
below the green trail; below, engraved drapery
swags linking four ovals, the two larger
enclosing a profile wreathed head and the
monogram 'PS', the two smaller enclosing
oval paterae; the lower bowl with cut relief
diamonds below semicircular arches and
short concave flutes.
h. 18.3 cm (a); 18.5 cm (b)

a) **Lady Lever Art Gallery, Port Sunlight LG5**
   W. Harding bequest, 1936.

b) **Williamson Art Gallery, Birkenhead 2288**
   W. Harding bequest, 1936.

Refs: Harding (1925) no 99.

England or Ireland
c1790 - 1810

E60
TURNOVER RIM BOWL

Colourless glass. The stem an inverted baluster. Cut; the body with a band of shallow lozenges above a band of relief diamonds and a double row of shallow lozenges; the rim with a band of relief diamonds edged with a row of small flutes; on the edge of the foot are narrow flutes.
h. 27.4 cm

Williamson Art Gallery, Birkenhead 2283
W. Harding bequest, 1936.
Harding Collection label on base, also a loan label inscribed 'Harding'.

Refs: Harding (1925) no 55.

Ireland
c1800

E61
CIRCULAR BOWL

Colourless glass. The stem with a central knop, the foot square. Cut; the bowl with a band of relief diamonds and leaflets above flutes crossed by two narrow horizontal grooves; the rim with slices and scalloped edge
h. 24.1 cm

Lady Lever Art Gallery, Port Sunlight
W. Harding bequest, 1936.
Harding Collection label on base, no 116.

Refs: Harding (1925) no 116.

Ireland
c1790 - 1800

E62
DECANTER

Colourless glass. The body with mould-blown flutes; the stopper of circular wafer form. On the neck three milled rings. Wheel-engraved, the upper body with a vesica motif punctuated with stars, the neck with a ring of dots. The base has a moulded inscription: 'CORK GLASS CO.'
h. (with stopper) 24.4 cm

Williamson Art Gallery, Birkenhead 2282
W. Harding bequest, 1936; from the Graydon Stannus collection.

Refs: Harding (1925) no 16.

Ireland: Cork Glass Co., Cork
c1800

E63
PUNCH BOWL AND COVER

Colourless glass. Cut; the bowl and cover with an all-over design of relief diamonds, the foot star cut, and a star on the flattened knop of the cover.
h. 31.5 cm

Manchester City Art Galleries 1920.1016
Lloyd Roberts bequest, 1920.

England or Ireland
c1820

E64
PAIR OF CANDELABRA

Colourless glass with opaque blue glass base.
Four branches on a pedestal base, two
branches supporting candleholders, two
supporting canopies and spear-shaft lustres;
a central spear-shaft lustre supporting a
canopy with a pineapple finial and three-
fold lustre chain. Cut; the branches notched,
the candleholders with diamonds and scalloped
rims, the canopies likewise. The blue glass
base mounted with gilt rams' heads, laurel
swags and paterae.
h. 76 cm

Oldham Art Gallery 17.55/3 and 4
From E.E. Cook via the National Art
Collections Fund, 1955.

England
c1780

94

E65
CANDELABRUM

Colourless glass with blue jasper ware base.
Five branches, two supporting candleholders,
two supporting spear-shaft lustres with
canopies and dangling lustres, one supporting
a three-fold lustre chain; central spear-shaft
lustre supporting a canopy, pineapple finial
and four lustre chains. Cut; the canopies and
candleholders scalloped and diamond-cut.
The blue jasper base with applied white
reliefs and gilt mounts.
h. 78 cm

Oldham Art Gallery 17.55/1
From E.E. Cook via the National Art
Collections Fund, 1955.

England
c1790

E66
PAIR OF CANDLESTICKS

Colourless glass. The stem with small inverted
baluster and base knop above a tall inverted
baluster. Cut; the stem with flutes and
diamonds, the nozzle with relief diamonds
and a scalloped edge; on the socket concave
diamonds and on the foot relief diamonds and
a scalloped edge.
h. (without nozzle) 23.2 cm

Manchester City Art Galleries 1920.980
Lloyd Roberts bequest, 1920.

England or Ireland
1780 - 1800

E67

THREE CANDLESTICKS

(a)
Colourless glass. The stem with two angular knops. Cut; the stem with relief diamonds, the socket diamond faceted, on the foot a wave pattern and a scalloped edge.
h. 24.6 cm

Merseyside County Museums 1978.374.6a
W. Harding bequest, 1936.

Refs: Harding (1925) no 18.

England
c1760 - 1780

(b)
Colourless glass. The stem multi-knopped. Cut; the stem and socket faceted, the foot with relief diamonds and a scalloped edge.
h. 24 cm

Merseyside County Museums 1978.374.6b
W. Harding bequest, 1936.

Refs: Harding (1925) no 28.

England
c1750 - 1780

(c)
Colourless glass. The stem straight with rounded knop at either end. Cut; the stem with facets and notches, the knops diamond cut; the socket diamond faceted, the foot with lozenges and lunar slices and a slightly scalloped edge.
h. 26 cm

Merseyside County Museums 1978.374.6c
W. Harding bequest, 1936.

Refs: Harding (1925) no 27.

England
c1750 - 1780

E68
PAIR OF CANDLESHADES

Colourless glass. Open at both ends, the rim
and foot flared. Cut; the body with all-over
flat diamonds, those in the central section
cross-cut; the rim bevelled and scalloped.
h. 54 cm

**Merseyside County Museums 1978.374
1a and b**
W. Harding bequest, 1936; from the
Graydon Stannus collection.

Refs: Harding (1925) no 96.

Ireland
c1800

E69
CRUET SET

Colourless glass; silver frame and mounts.
The set contains two cruets with silver covers
and handles, two mustard pots on pedestal
bases with silver lids, four bottles with glass
stoppers, silver mounted, all on a boat-
shaped silver stand. Cut; the upper bodies
with a band of relief diamonds and scallops,
the lower with vertical facets, the feet faceted
and scalloped; the bottles have faceted
stoppers. The silver frame hallmarked for
Daniel Pontifex, London 1794/5.
h. 27.2 cm; width (of frame) 37.5 cm

Manchester City Art Galleries 1920.1205
Lloyd Roberts bequest, 1920.

England: possibly London
1794 or 1795

Glass of the Nineteenth Century

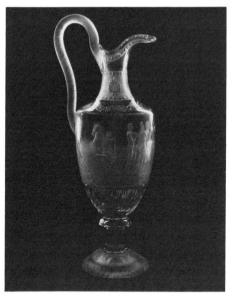

From about 1800, and particularly from about 1840, glassmakers became increasingly international in outlook. In this section therefore is described the glass of several European countries: France, Bohemia, Venice and Great Britain. Venetian nineteenth century glass has affinities with the art glass of other countries but is included here as it also represents a revival of traditional Venetian work.

F1
DECANTER JUG

Colourless glass, crystal. Cut and wheel-engraved. On the neck, between palmettes, the crowned Arms of Napoleon and the inscription 'QUIRIN GRAVEUR'; on the shoulder a running scroll framing a cartouche with the inscription 'orbi et sibi Imperat'. The body with Napoleon at Austerlitz; a trophy of arms rests on a pedestal with the inscription 'VICIT ET PEPERCIT AUSTERLITZ'; below, a border of palmettes and serpentine mitre cuts. The stem facet and flute cut; the foot with palmettes and bright engraved leaf ornament. Snake handle, cut and engraved. Stopper missing.
h. 37.3 cm

Manchester City Art Galleries 1917.681
Leicester Collier bequest, 1917.

France
c1805 - 1810

F2
BEAKER

Colourless glass. Cut, wheel-engraved and
stained. On the bowl one main and four
subsidiary panels with roundels above and
mitre and star cut squares below; at the base
of the bowl convex flutes. The main panel
six-sided; stained yellow and engraved with
a horse leaping a fallen tree; the squares
below stained blue. Stem faceted and foot
fluted with star and fan cut ornament beneath.
h. 16.5 cm

Pilkington Glass Museum 1978.18
Bought, 1978.

Bohemia: engraving attributed to Karel
Pfohl (1829 - 1894)
c1850

F3
EWER

Opalescent glass. Blown in ribbed mould
and wrythen. Rim cut with shears and tooled
to form scroll at either side; foot with
wrythen ribs, folded under. Between rim and
handle an applied combed scroll; the handle
of opalescent glass cased in colourless glass,
in the form of a dragon; pincered trail along
back; applied wings, legs and tail, the legs
combed, the wings and tail pincered.
h. 34.6 cm

Blackburn Museum and Art Gallery 191
Probably bought, perhaps in 1888.

Venice: probably Antonio Salviati
c1880

Note: The sole museum accession record of
Venetian glass is for October 1888 (1888.37);
'Venetian glass. Salisbury and Hamer, £2.2.6.'

F4
JUG

Opalescent glass. Blown in ribbed mould.
Rim with colourless trail, handle edged with
colourless glass and applied colourless lion
mask prunt at its base; foot folded under. The
whole splashed with ruby red and avventurine.
h. 32.5 cm

Blackburn Museum and Art Gallery 189
Probably bought, perhaps in 1888 (see note
on F3).

Venice: probably Antonio Salviati
c1880

F5
WINEGLASS

Opalescent glass. Blown in ribbed mould and
wrythen. The upper stem with incised twist
circlet set with two white flowers above a
third; the lower stem including a hollow
inverted baluster with applied, pincered wings;
the foot with wrythen ribs, folded under.
h. 23.8 cm

Blackburn Museum and Art Gallery 188
Probably bought, perhaps in 1888 (see note
on F3).

Venice: probably Antonio Salviati
c1880

F6
BOWL

Colourless glass, the bowl and foot in 'retorti' technique with avventurine included. Rim of bowl incurved; handles of pale bluish glass, avventurine splashed, in the form of winged grotesque horses. The stem of colourless glass with applied dolphins in pale bluish glass, avventurine splashed; the foot folded over.
h. 26.4 cm; d. approx 26.9 cm

Blackburn Museum and Art Gallery 190
Bought from Salviati & Co. Two labels, partly damaged, on the base. On one: 'Dr A...' and 'N.F. VENEZIA' printed, with '2/T v' and 'Stoff 12' (?) in ink. On the other 'SALVIATI AND CO. .. St. W' printed, with '£3.3.0.' in ink.

Venice: Antonio Salviati
c1865 - 1880

F7
TAZZA

Opalescent and colourless glass. The bowl opalescent with crimped rim, folded over; the stem colourless with hollow ribbed and knopped component over a solid plain part; four applied colourless wings with pincered crestings. Opalescent foot, folded under. Powdered gilding on bowl, stem and foot. Repaired.
h. 15.3 cm

Liverpool University G12
Sir Sydney Jones bequest, 1947.

Venice: perhaps Antonio Salviati
c1880

F8
WINEGLASS

Colourless glass. The bowl in 'retorti'
technique with twists of avventurine. The
stem in the form of a dolphin, hollow and
ribbed, with applied and pinched mouth, tail
and fins; below, a hollow ribbed baluster, the
whole stem with powdered gilding. Foot in
'retorti' technique as the bowl; folded under.
Repaired.
h. 23.4 cm

Liverpool University G13
Sir Sydney Jones bequest, 1947.

Venice: probably Antonio Salviati
c1870 - 1880

F9
WINEGLASS

Colourless glass. The bowl in 'retorti'
technique, the twists alternately white and
avventurine. The stem in the form of a swan,
hollow ribbed, with applied and pinched
wings, tail, head and feet; below, a hollow
ribbed baluster, the whole stem with
powdered gilding. Foot in 'retorti' technique
as the bowl; folded under. Repaired.
h. 23.4 cm

Liverpool University G18
Sir Sydney Jones bequest, 1947.

Venice: probably Antonio Salviati
c1870 - 1880

F10
WINEGLASS

Colourless glass. Cut and engraved. The bowl
with a crowned double monogram 'AA' and a
running scroll of roses and buds, thistles and
shamrocks; seven short flutes at the base.
The stem an opaque twist with seven flutes,
the foot with a forty-eight point star. On the
foot in diamond point, 'July 30 1846 ALBERT
DOCK'.
h. 14.3 cm

Merseyside County Museums 20.1.87 1-8
Given by the Rev. W. Bramley Moore, 1887.

England
1845 - 1846

Note: A museum catalogue card notes this as
one of 'eight specimens of glass used by His
Royal Highness Prince Albert K.G. at the
opening of the Albert Docks, Liverpool, July
1846'. Only this glass apparently survives.

F11
DECANTER

Pale yellow opaline glass. Transfer printed in
black with comic figures forming the word
'RUM' within the framework of a fruiting
vine; reverse, a bunch of grapes. On the base
is a transfer printed in black: 'RICHARDSON'S
VITRIFIED' on a scroll amid vine branches.

h. 31.8 cm

Pilkington Glass Museum, St Helens 1976/6
Bought, 1976.

England: W.H.B. and J. Richardson, Wordsley
c1850

F12
GOBLET

Colourless glass. Wheel-engraved, partly
corked and polished. The bowl with a snake
coiled around a tree in which is a nest of five
eggs with a bird approaching from either side;
reverse, a plant, perhaps deadly nightshade.
h. 15.4 cm

**Harris Museum and Art Gallery, Preston
DRT 130**
H.J. Taylor Collection; gift, 1945/6.

Great Britain
c1860

F13
GOBLET

Colourless glass. Wheel-engraved and cut; the
bowl with stags in a landscape, the stem fluted.
h. 17.7 cm

Salford Museum and Art Gallery 1865-2689
Acquired 1865.

Great Britain
c1860 - 1865

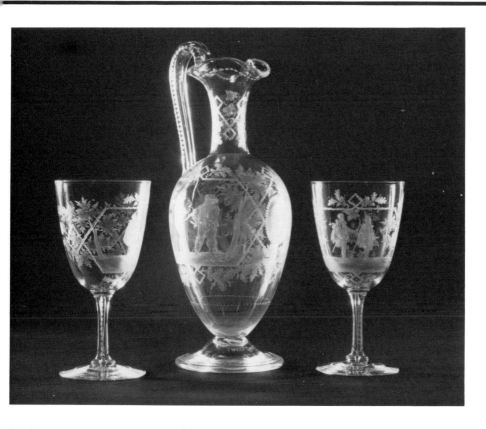

F14
WATER JUG AND PAIR OF GOBLETS

(a)
JUG

Colourless glass. The handle with applied lion mask terminal at its base and central air column, the foot folded over. Acid-etched in outline and white acid and wheel-engraved; bust of Shakespeare in rustic oak frame with a scene from Twelfth Night; engraved balls on rim, handle edge and fold of foot. Etched on foot: 'TWELFTH NIGHT ACT III SCENE IV'. h. 29.2 cm

(b)
GOBLETS

Colourless glass. The stems with central air columns, the feet flat. Decoration as for the jug, with other scenes from Twelfth Night and floral sprays; engraved balls on stems and feet. h. 16.5 cm

Pilkington Glass Museum, St Helens 1978.4 1-3
Bought, 1978.

England: Stourbridge
c1870 - 1875

F15
GOBLET

Colourless glass. Wheel-engraved and cut. The bowl with inscription 'David and Sarah Plinston, Warrington 1873' in a wreath and a view of Warrington Town Hall framed by trees; inscriptions 'NEW TOWN HALL WARRINGTON' and 'Opened June 20th 1873'. The stem facet cut and fluted; on the foot a leafy circlet.
h. 22.4 cm

Warrington Museum, Alderman Plinston loan
On loan from Miss M. Plinston.

England: probably T. Robinson & Co., Warrington
1873

F16
COMPORT

Colourless glass. Press-moulded, the stem with seams from a three-piece mould. Patterned in imitation of cut glass, the bowl and foot with alternate panels and blazes, the hollow stem with flutes and facets. Design Registry mark for January 2nd 1882 inside the bowl.
h. 20.6 cm; d. 26.8 cm

Manchester City Art Galleries 1977.29
Bought, 1977.

Refs: Pottery Gazette 1883, supplement: Comport No 66 from the 'Duchess Service'.

England: Molineaux, Webb & Co, Manchester
1882 or later

F17
VASE

Colourless glass. The bowl circular at the base, the rim of flattened oval plan. Wheel-engraved in 'rock crystal' technique, brush polished; the bowl with Chinese bat motif and floral scrolls; rim and foot with geometric ornament.
h. 7.8 cm

Pilkington Glass Museum, St Helens 1967.7
Bought, 1976.

England: Thos. Webb & Sons, Stourbridge 1884 or later

Note: the shape and ornament are very close to pattern 14072 in the Webb factory pattern books, dated 1884.

F18
PAIR OF WATER JUGS AND FOUR GOBLETS

(a)
JUGS

Colourless glass. Cut and wheel-engraved.
The neck with notched flutes; on the shoulder the monogram 'JB' with leaf sprays either side. The body has vertical panels of notched relief diamonds and alternate panel motifs with two diagonal friezes of fruit and floral engraving crossing the latter; on the lower body raised ovals on a ground of relief diamonds, and swirled mitre cutting and a smaller repeat of the main body panels. Behind the handle, engraved leaf sprays within a line border. The foot fluted, on four triple-lobed extensions cut with fine relief diamonds.
h. 34.7 cm

(b)
GOBLETS

Colourless glass. Body and foot cut in manner of jugs; the stem fluted and faceted.
h. 19.9 cm

Rochdale Museum
Probably given by the Bright family in 1924.

Refs: Catalogue of the John Bright Memorial Exhibition, Rochdale Art Gallery 1925, No 6

England: F. and C. Osler, Birmingham 1883

Note: The presentation case for these glasses is labelled 'F. and C. OSLER, Glass Manufacturers, Birmingham'. The case was presented by the Birmingham Liberal Association to John Bright M.P. (1811 - 1889) to mark his twenty-fifth year as a Member of Parliament for the Borough; a dessert service was also presented, the centrepiece to which is in the Rochdale Museum.

108

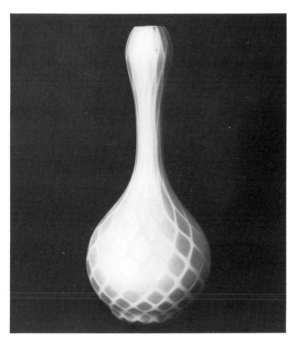

F19
VASE

Overlay glass, transparent pale blue on opaque white. Diamond air-lock pattern, with satin finish.
h. 25.5 cm

Merseyside County Museums 50.30.312
B. Read gift, 1950.

England: probably Stevens and Williams, Brierley Hill
c1885

F20
JUG

Colourless glass. Wheel-engraved; portrait of a man at a desk, within a wreath, flanked by views of two chapels, inscribed 'WESLEY CHAPEL, BEWSEY RD' and 'WESLEYAN CHAPEL, BOLD ST'. Leaf border below rim.
h. 20.1 cm

Warrington Museum 25.60
Mrs F.C. Richardson gift, 1960.

England: probably T. Robinson & Co., Warrington
c1875 - 1890

Note: the portrait is said to be of Mr T. Richardson, a prominent Warrington Methodist in the mid-nineteenth century.

ART GLASS OF THE LATE 19TH AND EARLY 20TH CENTURY
i) Continental Europe

G1
VASE

Opaque cream-coloured glass overlaid with dark inky blue. Etched and carved in cameo technique with a lakeside landscape of pine forests. Signed 'Gallé' in cameo.
h. 45 cm

Pilkington Glass Museum, St Helens 1966.9
Bought, 1966.

France: Emile Gallé, Nancy
c1900

Glass of factories tending to specialise in decorative pieces rather than tableware. The groups described are:
i) Continental
ii) English
iii) American.
Of the American group the Tiffany glass is dated according to the scheme adopted in the Chrysler Museum, Norfolk, catalogue of Tiffany glass (1978).

G2
VASE

Iridescent lustre glass. The shoulder an opaque apricot lustre with mother-of-pearl iridescent trails, the body of ivory lustre with greenish gold swirling trails; a thick overlay of purplish-black marbled lustre on the base section.
h. 18 cm

Manchester Polytechnic 50.1902
Purchased Liberty & Co, 1902; two labels on the base, written in ink: 'Loetz, Bohemian' and 'E 1484 42/-'.

Bohemia: Loetz Witwe, Klostermühle
c1900

G3
DECANTER

Colourless glass. Mould-blown in ribbed
mould, then free-blown; the sides pushed in.
A colourless trail on the neck; stopper of
'poppy-head' form.
h. (with stopper) 31.7 cm

Manchester City Art Galleries 1918.198
Horsfall Collection.

London: J. Powell & Sons
Late C19

G4
WINEGLASS

Transparent pale turquoise glass. Mould-
blown in ribbed mould (bowl and foot); stem
of hollow wrythen ribbed form with trailed
wings.
h. 19 cm

Manchester City Art Galleries 1918.239
Horsfall Collection.

London: J. Powell & Sons
Late C19

G5
FLUTE

Colourless glass with opalescence. Bowl
tooled to octagonal rim form; pinched
quatrefoil stem.
h. 20.9 cm

Manchester Polytechnic
Bought between 1902 and 1910.

London: J. Powell & Sons
Late C19

G6
FLUTE

Transparent pale green glass. Stem of
pinched quatrefoil shape with four tiny
applied bosses, each nicked diagonally.
h. 22.9 cm

Manchester Polytechnic
Bought between 1902 and 1910.

London: J. Powell & Sons
Late C19

G7
WINEGLASS

Transparent pale green glass. Rim of bowl
crimped, the stem with two deeply indented
twists each with enclosed air column.
h. 20.7 cm

Manchester Polytechnic
Bought between 1902 and 1910.

London: J. Powell & Sons
Late C19

G8
TAZZA

Opalescent glass. Rim of bowl crimped, the
stem with two deeply indented twists, each
with enclosed air column.
h. 17.5 cm

Manchester Polytechnic
Bought, probably in 1902.

London: J. Powell & Sons
Late C19

G9
BOWL

Pale green glass with cobalt blue overlay.
Irregular trails of opaque white marvered
between the layers; scattered metallic
inclusions. On bronze stand.
h. (the glass) 26.9 cm

Manchester Polytechnic 4.1903
Bought from W.A.S. Benson & Co, London,
1903.

London: J. Powell & Sons
c1900

G10
GOBLET

Transparent pale green glass. Stem drawn
from the bowl. Two groups of whitish-blue
trails, marvered, from the bottom of the stem
to near the bowl rim, in stylised flower forms;
bowl and stem sprinkled with avventurine.
h. 26.9 cm

Manchester Polytechnic
Bought between 1902 and 1910.

Refs: The Studio Vol XVIII, 1899, p252
(illus. of this or similar glass).

London: J. Powell & Sons
c1895 - 1900

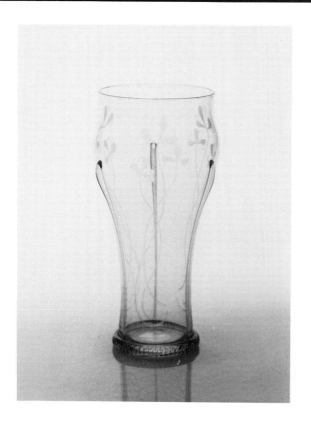

G11
BEAKER

Transparent pale green glass. Three vertical
trails of pale green and milled trail around the
base. Wheel-engraved flowers with stylised
interlace stems between the trails.
h. 17.3 cm

Manchester Polytechnic
Probably bought from J. Powell & Sons,
September 1903. ('1 engraved vase, fruit,
with sea green tears and full at base' - Museum
Stock Journal).

London: J. Powell & Sons
c1900

G12
TWO HANDLED BEAKER

Transparent pale green glass. Applied handles
with pincered trails. Thin circuit trail around
lower body and thick milled trail around base;
two opposed patterned prunts. Wheel-
engraved inscription below rim 'EDWARDUS
VII'. D'I. GRA'. BR'. OM'. RE'. E'. IN'.
IMP'.' Inscription 'KING'S CUP' round one
prunt and stylised floral decoration round
the other.
h. 16 cm

Manchester Polytechnic 89.1903
Bought from J. Powell & Sons, 1903.

London: J. Powell & Sons
1902 - 1903

116

G13
DECANTER

Iridescent lustre glass, orange/gold opaque
fading to cream near neck; decorated with
wave-like design in orange/gold/green lustre
streaked with black. Signed and numbered
on base 'L.C. Tiffany Favrile D 947'.
Stopper also numbered.
h. 32 cm

Haworth Art Gallery, Accrington
Joseph Briggs gift, 1933.

Labels: The 1894 Tiffany Glass and
Decorating Co. label, black monogram on
white, and hand written label '$40' on the
base.

New York: L.C. Tiffany
1895

G14
VASE

Iridescent lustre glass, opaque dull olive green.
Peacock blue iridescent lily pad and tendril
decoration. Etched on base 'L.C. Tiffany
Favrile Q 9858'.
h. 18 cm

Haworth Art Gallery, Accrington
Joseph Briggs gift, 1933.

The 1904 Tiffany Co. label, printed in black,
on the base.

New York: L.C. Tiffany
1902

G15
GOBLET

Iridescent lustre glass, gold with purple
iridescence. Base initialled L.C.T. T 3893.
h. 22.2 cm

Manchester Polytechnic
Bought probably in 1903, from Tiffany & Co.

New York: L.C. Tiffany
1903

G16
FLOWER FORM VASE

Iridescent lustre glass, gold with purple/pink
iridescence. The body slightly ribbed. Base
initialled L.C.T. W 8594.
h. 19.1 cm

Manchester Polytechnic
Bought apparently in 1903, from Tiffany & Co.

Remains of the 1904 L.C. Tiffany Co. label,
printed in black, on the base.

New York: L.C. Tiffany
1905

Note: The only record of acquisition of
Tiffany glass by the Manchester Polytechnic
is for October 1903. In the Museum
Accessions book is noted under No 55.1903
'Ornamental glass irridescent [sic]; various
shapes' bought from Tiffany & Co. This
glass (G16) should, according to the dating
method adopted, date from 1905.

G17
PAPERWEIGHT VASE

Transparent red glass with slight interior
iridescence. Internal decoration of lily leaves
and trailing tendrils in green and brown.
Etched on base 'L.C. Tiffany Favrile Y 9190'.
h. 18.8 cm

Haworth Art Gallery, Accrington
Joseph Briggs gift, 1933.

New York: L.C. Tiffany
1905

G18
CAMEO VASE

Semi-opaque green/grey glass overlaid with
dark green and white. Etched and carved
lily-like leaves and white sprigs of blossom.
Etched on base 'L.C. Tiffany Favrile 5015 C'.
h. 24.4 cm

Haworth Art Gallery, Accrington
Joseph Briggs gift, 1933.

Labels: the 1904 L.C. Tiffany Co. label, in
green and gold, and handwritten label '$50',
on the base.

New York: L.C. Tiffany
1908

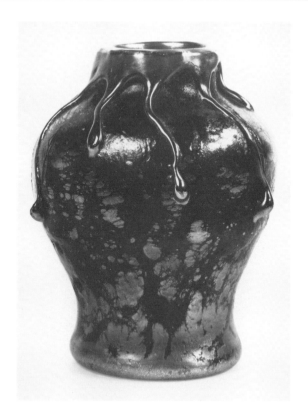

G19
LAVA VASE

Lava glass, opaque mottled purple and blue flecked with gold, with patchy iridescence; around the rim a band of thick gold lustre, falling in trails down the body. On base 'L.C. Tiffany Favrile 9926 C'.
h. 15.4 cm

Haworth Art Gallery, Accrington
Joseph Briggs gift, 1933.

The 1904 L.C. Tiffany Co. label, printed black on white, on the base.

New York: L.C. Tiffany
1908

G20
PAPERWEIGHT VASE

Colourless glass with faint interior iridescence. Internal decoration of trailing lily pads and tendrils, in deep apricot yellow and yellow-green. Etched on base 'L.C. Tiffany Favrile 5033 E'.
h. 43.9 cm

Haworth Art Gallery, Accrington
Joseph Briggs gift, 1933.

The 1904 L.C. Tiffany Co. label, printed black on white, on the base.

New York: L.C. Tiffany
1910

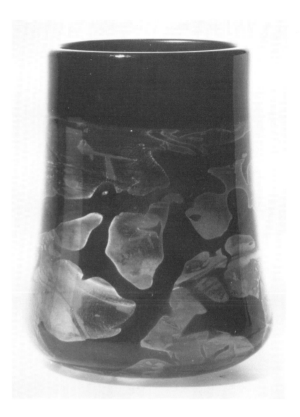

G21
PAPERWEIGHT VASE

Opaque marbleised glass, green flecked with
yellow and red, below transparent straw-
coloured glass encasing cream and yellow
opaque swirls. A scrolling pattern in black
on the shoulder. Etched on base 'L.C.
Tiffany Favrile 6415 T'.
h. 9.8 cm

Haworth Art Gallery, Accrington
Joseph Briggs gift, 1933.

The 1904 L.C. Tiffany Co. label, printed green
on gold, on the base.

New York: L.C. Tiffany
1915

G22
PAPERWEIGHT VASE

Transparent pale green glass with slight blue/
green iridescence; a deep band of emerald
green opaque glass round the rim. Internal
decoration of marbled pattern in greens and
yellows. Etched on base 'L.C. Tiffany Favrile
1139 L Exhibition Piece'.
h. 12.7 cm

Haworth Art Gallery, Accrington
Joseph Briggs gift, 1933.

New York: L.C. Tiffany
1917

G23
CYPRIOTE VASE

Opaque dull grey glass with pitted surface.
Decoration of streaks of purple-blue lustre,
blistered. Etched on base 'L.C.T. 3323 P'.
h. 12.7 cm

Haworth Art Gallery, Accrington
Joseph Briggs gift, 1933.

New York: L.C. Tiffany
1921

G24
VASE

Iridescent lustre glass, greenish gold with
purple iridescence. Gold lustre inside neck
and deep purple iridescent rim. Decoration
of swirled streaks of lavender blue. Etched
'Quezal' on base.
h. 18 cm

Pilkington Glass Museum, St Helens 1974.11
Given by G. McKinley, 1974.

New York: Quezal Art Glass & Decorating Co

Early C20

Bibliography

The bibliography is composed entirely of works cited in the catalogue.

AKERMAN (1855) J.Y. Akerman. Remains of Pagan Saxondom. London, 1855.

BARAG (1975) D.P. Barag. 'Rod-formed Kohl Tubes of the Mid-First Millenium B.C.', in Journal of Glass Studies, vol. XVII, 1975, pp 23-26.

BRUNTON (1930) G. Brunton. Qau and Badari III. London, 1930.

CHRYSLER (1978) P.E. Doros. The Tiffany Collection of the Chrysler Museum at Norfolk. Norfolk, Virginia, 1978.

GATTY (1879) C.T. Gatty. Catalogue of the Mayer Collection, part I. London, 1879.

GATTY (1883) C.T. Gatty. Catalogue of the Mediaeval and Later Antiquities contained in the Mayer Museum. Liverpool, 1883.

HARDEN (1967-8) D.B. Harden. 'Late Roman Wheel Inscribed Glasses with Double Line Letters', in Kölner Jahrbuch für vor-und Frühgeschichte, vol. 9, 1967-8, p 52.

HARDEN (1969) D.B. Harden. 'Ancient Glass I', in Archaeological Journal, vol. CXXV, London, 1969, pp 46 ff.

HARDEN (1972) D.B. Harden. 'Ancient Glass III', in Archaeological Journal, vol. CXXVIII, London, 1972, pp 44 ff.

'HARDING' (1925) Old Irish Glass. The Walter Harding Collection. Privately published, 1925 (reprint 1930).

HOBSON (1928) R.L. Hobson. Chinese Porcelain and Wedgwood Pottery. A Record of the Collections in the Lady Lever Art Gallery. (The Leverhulme Art Collections vol. II). London, 1928.

HURST (1968) R. Hurst. 'Rare glass from the City of Liverpool Museums', in Liverpool Bulletin, Museums No., vol. 14, 1968, pp 16-31.

GS Journal of Glass Studies

MAYER (1852) J. Mayer. Catalogue of Egyptian Museum. Liverpool, 1852.

NOLTE	(1968)	B. Nolte. Die Glasgefässe im alten Ägypten. Berlin, 1968.
PETRIE	(1889)	W.M. Flinders Petrie. Hawara, Biahmu and Arsinöe. London, 1889.
PETRIE	(1891)	W.M. Flinders Petrie. Illahun, Kahun and Gurob 1889-90. London, 1891.
PETRIE	(1906)	W.M. Flinders Petrie. Hyksos and Israelite Cities. London, 1906.
PRICE	(1979)	J. Price. 'Glass of the Roman Empire in Museums in Britain', in the 8th Bulletin de l'Association Internationale pour l'Histoire du Verre. To be published 1979.
SAMS	(1839)	Egyptian Antiquities from the collection of Joseph Sams. London, 1839.
SMITH	(n.d.)	C.R. Smith. Collectanea Antiqua, vol. III. Printed for subscribers only, n.d. (c1854-1855).
SMITH	(1856)	C.R. Smith (ed). Inventorium Sepulchrale. London, 1856.
TSGT		Transactions of the Society of Glass Technology.
THORPE	(1929)	W.A. Thorpe. A History of English and Irish Glass. London, 1929.
THORPE	(1930)	W.A. Thorpe. 'English Glass at the Manchester City Art Gallery', in The Collector, vol. XI Sept-Dec. 1930, pp 89-96.
THORPE	(1935)	W.A. Thorpe. 'The Roscoe Collection of English Glass', in The Connoisseur, Oct. 1935, pp 205-209.
THORPE	(1938)	W.A. Thorpe. 'Prelude to European Cut Glass', in TSGT XXII, 1938, pp 5-37.

Index

Richardson, Mrs F.C.	F20
Robinow, Mr	A45
Rochdale Museum	E32, F18
Rolfe, W.H.	B1, B5, B6
Roscoe, W.M.	D29, D33, D34, D36, D37, D39, D40, E4, E5, E6, E11, E14, E15, E22, E23, E24, E25, E26, E29, E31, E33, E34, E37, E50
Sale, J.	D25
Salford Museum and Art Gallery	E40, F13
Sams, Joseph	A2
Shaw, J.	A28
Stitt, J. Carlton	C2b and c
Taylor, Dr H.J.	E7, E8, E9, E10, F12
Towneley Hall, Burnley	E16, E17
Tylecote, Prof. F.	D32, E36
University of Liverpool	F7, F8, F9
Wareham, Mr	D14
Warrington Museum and Art Gallery	F15, F20
Williamson Art Gallery, Birkenhead	D18, D19, D27, E57, E59b, E60, E62
Williamson, J.	D18, D19, D27

Lenders

The following kindly agreed to lend glass to this exhibition:

Abbot Hall Art Gallery, Kendal
Blackburn Museum and Art Gallery
Bolton Museum and Art Gallery
Grosvenor Museum and Art Gallery, Chester
Harris Museum and Art Gallery, Preston
Haworth Art Gallery, Accrington
Lady Lever Art Gallery, Port Sunlight
The Lord Newton
Lyme Park, Disley (The National Trust)
Manchester City Art Galleries
The Manchester Museum
Manchester Polytechnic, Faculty of Arts
Merseyside County Museums
Oldham Art Gallery and Museum
Pilkington Glass Museum, St Helens
Rochdale Museum
Salford Museum and Art Gallery
Towneley Hall, Burnley
University of Liverpool Art Gallery
Warrington Museum and Art Gallery
Williamson Art Gallery and Museum, Birkenhead

Particular thanks are due to those members of staff in the above institutions who so readily made glass and records available for study and who provided information on their collections.